"Can These Bones Come to Life?": Insights from Re-construction, Re-enactment, and Re-creation

Volume II
High in Protean Content

Papers Sponsored by the Higgins Armory Museum and the Oakeshott Institute at the International Medieval Congress, Kalamazoo, MI, May 12–15, 2012

EDITED BY MICHAEL A. CRAMER

SERIES EDITORS:
KEN MONDSCHEIN AND MICHAEL A. CRAMER

Wheaton, Illinois

Freelance Academy Press, Inc., Wheaton, IL 60189
www.freelanceacademypress.com

Printed in the United States of America
by Publishers' Graphics

21 20 19 18 17 16 15 14 13 12 1 2 3 4 5

ISBN 978-1-937439-14-9

Library of Congress Control Number: 2014932145

CONTENTS

INTRODUCTION

Michael A. Cramer

In *Imagining Robin Hood,* A. J. Pollard opined that "history is nothing if not messing about with the past."[1] That's what this book is about.

At the International Congress of Medieval Studies at Kalamazoo in 2007, Ken Mondschein organized a pair of panels, both called " 'Can These Bones come To Life?': Insights from Re-Construction, Re-enactment, and Re-creation." At one of these panels, Ramon Martinez, a professional fencing teacher whose biography on his website describes him a "traditional master of arms,"[2] presented a paper in which he argued that no one should undertake to study the *Fechtbücher* (medieval fighting manuals) unless under the tutelage of a fencing master. His argument was that the Fechtbücher are built upon a foundation of principles of movement, distance and defense that can only be understood after years of rigorous study, and that simply studying and trying to re-create their techniques without the guidance of a master will lead to misinterpretation. At the time I argued that, in addition to being self-serving (which he was happy to admit), it also was short sighted, because most of the work of the last twenty years in re-discovering and interpreting the Fechtbücher has been done by enthusiastic amateurs, not by masters. Unfortunately, those same enthusiastic amateurs who have brought the Fechtbücher to life often do not have the training to seek out primary source material, translate, or critically analyze it, or, for that matter, to write a well structured and well sourced piece of research. So the next year I presented a response paper with my own self-serving argument that study of the Fechtbücher should only be carried out under the tutelage of qualified academics. It was not well received among the wider historical martial arts crowd.

There is another argument to be made, however, and it is at the heart of Ken's project. The Fechtbücher have been largely ignored by professional scholars up until now, and this is a mistake. There is a wealth of source material out there in the Fechtbücher, dozens of documents in several different languages that represent a rich trove of cultural history as well as fighting techniques. Except for the work of Sydney Anglo, these books have largely been passed over by Anglophone academics. It is the amateurs who have been dissecting and analyzing these books. These same enthusiastic amateurs and their friends have for the past fifty years been conducting some of the most interesting research in Medieval Studies, and performing some brilliant experiments in medieval technology and culture, under the large and somewhat contested umbrella of "medieval reenactment" (accompanying terms, such as re-creation or re-construction are also used but reenactment generally encompasses all of them in most discussions). Reenactment, an activity often mocked and scorned by medieval scholars, has over the last twenty years or so slowly started to creep into the academic fold, through the efforts of academics who came to medieval studies through their love of reenactment. Most of this convergence was accomplished in the study of material culture in groups such as DISTAFF and AVISTA, but has spread to other areas of study.

Part of Ken's purpose in organizing these panels was to bring the work being done in re-enactment to the notice of the Academy. As the project grew, it attracted scholars studying other attempts at re-creating the Middle Ages, including fashion designers, dance historians, musicians, archeologist, artisans, and literary critics, until it became a serious look at the possibilities available to scholars through various forms of "messing about with the past." This book is a direct result of these conference sessions, which have been held, in various forms, since 2005. In the years since, in collaboration with various sponsoring groups, Ken has been organizing panels at Kalamazoo and elsewhere, and I have been presenting at them. When Ken became a research fellow at the Higgins Armory in Worcester, MA, the Higgins became the sponsoring organization. Along the way, we teamed up with The Chicago Sword Guild, the Oakeshott Institute, and La Belle Compagnie, presenting papers on all areas of medieval reenactment. After five years of material we decided to publish proceedings of what we were doing. The first volume in this series, edited by Ken, was a collection of papers from earlier conferences. This second volume contains material from our sessions in 2012. Thirteen scholars presented as part of our series in 2012, in four sessions. Their work included demonstrations of combat techniques, slide shows, discussions, and the seven papers included here.

Russell Mitchell's paper "There is No True Art of the Sword" comes from a session organized by Annamaria Kovacs of the Oakeshott Institute. It is a response to a paper the prior year by Keith Alderson, and dovetailed with the demonstration that Keith and Greg Mele did in 2012, comparing techniques in Italian and German Fechtbücher. In his paper, Russ rebuts Keith's assertion that the German and Italian techniques are part of the same tradition.

The next three papers are from that year's "Bones" session. In " 'Forward Into the Past': Re-enactors, Professionals, and the quest for Authenticity," Lisa Evans explores some of the pitfalls and pleasures of combining scholarship and reenactment by looking at a collaborative attempt among scholars and embroiderers to reconstruct a seventeenth century jacket. In "Glass on Fire: Temperatures in Reconstructed Norse Bead Furnaces," Neil Peterson, of the Dark Ages Re-Creation Company, presents a technical examination of Viking-era bead making, looking at temperature drop-offs in re-constructed furnaces, and speculates on how this might affect bead manufacturing. Daryl Markowitz, a professional blacksmith, writes about a work of experimental archeology that he organized, an iron smelt using tenth-century technology that took place at the site of the Viking settlement in L'Anse Aux Meadows, Newfoundland, where evidence of smelting has been discovered, in a paper titled simply "An Iron Smelt in Vinland: An Experimental Investigation."

The final set of papers comes from a panel titled "High in Protean Content: Chivalry and Its Transformations," wherein presenters examined specific aspects of chivalry. In "The Chivalric Warrior as a Man of his Word," Steven Muhlberger proposes that there is a whole genre of chivalric literature built around the idea of the angry knight who has been prohibited for some reason from fulfilling a vow, and that this exposes and sometimes critiques knightly pride. In " 'Seeking That Which Cannot Be Found': The Use of Lancelot as Contemporary Social Commentary in *The Once and Future King,*" Emerson Storm Richards looks at how T.H. White melded together various source material in a commentary on the concept of chivalry, both modern and medieval. This section also includes my own paper, "Franchise and Chivalric Identity," in which I examine the contested virtue of franchise as an important element in the performance of chivalry.

As I write this introduction, the 2013 Congress has just ended, and many of us remarked on how well our project has succeeded. Whereas at one time re-enactors were asked (courteously) not to attend Kalamazoo, this past year that prejudice was buried. Reenactment activities were everywhere. La Belle Companie put on a demonstration of how a man should be armed—essentially an armored fashion show. There was a reconstruction of a judicial duel next door to an interactive panel on chant—un-intentionally creating a fight scene with a soundtrack. Daryl and Neil conducted an iron smelt out on the lawn over two days. Best of all, the beer and mead tasting was back. While enthusiastically sampling some excellent meads, we congratulated ourselves on having helped to spur this change forward. Papers from this conference will appear in Volume Three of this series.

Endnotes

1. A. J. Pollard, *Imagining Robin Hood* (New York: Routledge, 2004), 5.
2. http://martinez-destreza.com/Instructors, accessed June 17, 2013.

THERE IS NO ONE TRUE ART OF THE SWORD

Russell Mitchell

Recently, I was taken by surprise by what seems to be an acceptance in the scholarly community of the notion that there is "one art of the sword": that there is an essential unity to all European fencing. This came about after Keith Alderson's presentation, "'But One True Art of the Sword': Italian and German Longsword Techniques Compared," given at the 45th annual Conference on Medieval Studies at Kalamazoo, Michigan, in May 2010. This fine-sounding *topos* seems to have garnered wide acceptance of late, and it strikes me as an idea that needs to be addressed before it can take root and begin bearing unfortunate fruit. It seems quite clear to me that even a casual exegesis reveals that this notion is quite mistaken. Such a statement mistakes the rhetorical process of writing about swordplay, to the obscurement of differences in how various medieval people actually used swords—an understanding of which is crucial to any attempt to actually understand what (besides fencing with people and/or killing them) medieval man was actually doing when engaged in the subject. We do not find "one art" of the sword in medieval Europe: rather, there are consistent and significant differences found in posture, combative philosophy, technique, and even physical conditioning, all which must be taken into account if we are to gain a proper understanding of medieval swordplay.

On a literal level, we certainly don't see one art of the sword. In fact, there are two very distinct "arts" depicting swordplay that need to be addressed if one is to understand how the weapons were used. While medieval "fencing" manuscripts[1] are still generally known only to a specialist audience, medieval artwork describing combat are numerous and well known. There tends to be distinct differences between combat as depicted in most medieval artwork, and that shown in the various fencing manuscripts. Comparing the two suggests that most of our martial arts records were much more for play than for "earnest" fighting in battle.

Some years ago I was struck by what seemed to be a distinct difference between the postures generally shown in medieval fencing manuscripts, and the postures individual warriors were shown using in the general artwork of the period. Particularly, there seemed to be a notable break in the postures shown dating more or less from the adoption of rigid plate armor in the late fourteenth and fifteenth centuries. I hypothesized that both the lunge and the primary line of engagement[2] taken for granted in later fencing manuscripts were derived from the development of the rigid coat of plates and breastplate, which remove the option of using torsion in the upper body to generate power. Descriptions of power generation constitute a fairly advanced topic even among martial artists and athletes, but one can understand the difference by visualizing the difference in how the upper body of a modern fencer moves, when compared to that of a tennis player. Assuming that a modern fencer wasn't overburdened by weight, a rigid breastplate would not keep one from fencing well, and if light enough, might not hinder a fencer in the slightest. On the other hand, Serena Williams would be severely handicapped were she forced to wear a rigid breastplate, even a light one, while playing at Wimbledon.

The following data was presented during my presentation "How the Breastplate Created 'Fencing' " at the 43rd Medieval Congress at Kalamazoo in 2008, but as it is highly relevant to the current discussion, I need to discuss it here as well. In my previous presentation, as I tried to determine why there were such profound changes in medieval swordplay, seeming to begin more or less in the fourteenth century, I decided to lean on Nicolle's much-browsed but rarely-referenced *Arms and Armor of the Crusading Era*, while restricting myself solely to the first volume.[3] I did this for two reasons: Firstly, while the volume in question contains numerous minor artistic errors, these tend to be restricted to minor detail work around the edges. In terms of gesture, which is what this study requires, the quality seems to match the primary sources very well. Secondly, by not re-inventing the wheel, but instead relying on a previous study, other interested parties can double-check the work and make their own decisions as to whether the images were sufficiently representative for the thesis to be upheld. Eventually, my thesis was *not* upheld; while I remained convinced that there is a significant change in power generation which occurs at the end of the medieval period and into the Renaissance, the artistic artwork did not support the notion that there was a change in "line of engagement." I was unable to determine any universal "fighting geometry" in the High Middle Ages and earlier to speak of, and I turned down several offers to elaborate and publish the work as I became convinced that I had diagnosed a problem,[4] but not come up with any worthwhile solution to it.

The data, on the other hand, remains good, and Nicolle's work provides a good foundation for pursuing the work during the beginning of the period we are discussing. To continue into the later period when the transition for which we are looking would have occurred, I combined the medieval *fechtbuch* literature (which becomes available roughly from the beginning of the fourteenth century on, but particularly from the mid-to-late fifteenth century) with a number of well-known manuscript sources such as the Arthurian romance Yale 229 (late thirteenth century),[5] the Morgan Bible (mid-thirteenth century),[6] the *Life of Saint Edward the Confessor* (1250s),[7] the Holkham Picture Bible (mid-fourteenth century),[8] the copy of the *Grandes Chroniques de France* made for Charles V (end of the fourteenth century),[9] and the lavish Louis of Gruuthuse volumes of Froissart's *Chronicles* (end of the fifteenth century).[10]

Unfortunately, there is a giant methodological elephant in the room which must be addressed before we proceed, and that is the question of whether any of these images, made over a broad period of time, can be taken as lifelike in the absence of perspective, and knowing that artistic images may be employed as part of a convention, or in terms dictated by the artistic space. It is my contention that they can be, and indeed, unless obviously stylized, *must be.* While some medieval artwork is clearly conventionalized and made according to artistic style or fad, others seem life-like and plausible, and one should note that plenty of non-medieval art is quite lifelike without conforming to perspective. While it is true that medieval artwork does not approach images in quite the same way that a modern audience does, accustomed as we are to strict perspective and stop-motion imagery, some baseline assumption of reliability is the price of being able to engage in scholarly work with the sources at all.

It is my contention that the general tendency to dismiss images as "conventions" is actually *less* rigorous than taking them at face value. This is highly controversial. It is one thing to say, for instance, that a given posture is used as a convention to signify that the person shown is a knight. But why was *this* posture used for a given convention, and not *that* one? If we find that the posture in question, used to signify social status, is modified over time, that is important artistic information that needs to be addressed, rather than dismissed. Similarly, artistic space may dictate that a weapon is depicted in either a horizontal or vertical fashion. However, there are many ways in which this can be done, and any dismissal of a given figure under such circumstances needs to be justified, rather than merely asserted. Most importantly, in the absence of clearly contravening circumstances such as obvious stylization (one would not, for instance, use a figure from highly-formalized Anglo-Saxon artwork such as the Book of Kells for our current purposes), if one cannot accept images in medieval artwork in general as lifelike, upon what grounds does one accept that medieval artwork in any of the pre-perspective fencing manuals is lifelike, either? The "natural-ness" of a posture is an insufficient grounds on which to act, because it is simply a facile means to dismiss any counter-intuitive posture—its counterpart is simply the "No True Scotsman" logical fallacy by which one *asserts* that one posture is more lifelike than the other without a factual basis for doing so.[11] Similarly, we cannot hold a posture to be a "convention" of some other posture—such circular assertions are by nature unfalsifiable. At some point, we must assume that we can rely upon the artwork, however cautiously, or we are unable to proceed at all. Therefore, this study proceeds upon the scholarly assumption that one cannot dismiss any given image without justifying and defending that dismissal, and that the simple *assertion* of "convention" is insufficient grounds for doing so.

Methodological minefield thus addressed, let us return to the main topic. Out of the more than 800 sketches presented in Nicolle's work, combined with additional images from the above-mentioned manuscripts, 224 seemed relevant to the task at hand. As expected, a survey of the postures indicated show some overlaps with the earliest known *Fechtbuch*, Royal Armouries MS I.33, but otherwise represent a distinct break from the majority of the postures depicted once we enter into the general "Fechtbuch era" starting in the late fourteenth and early fifteenth centuries.

While every fighting system depends upon a series of stances of postures in order to enable one to perform the techniques that it teaches, one of the immediate yardsticks we can use to get a sense of how relevant a given manuscript was, would be to determine whether the postures in the one source are found elsewhere. In other words, do the fencing postures shown in the manuscripts appear within other pieces of medieval artwork which depict fencing in a context of combat, rather than of practice?

Of the six most common postures, only one of the standard postures with which we are familiar from the later *Fechtbücher* makes anything even vaguely resembling a common appearance, and that position is by no means the most commonly depicted posture. The fighting position in question is the generic and generalized high guard, which could plausibly also be interpreted as a Fourth Guard as shown in MS I.33, with the point and blade sloped distinctly backwards, though not consistently either up or down. A "true" (depending on one's school, of course) high guard, or the *turret* [12]as found within the messer fencing of Johannes Leckûchner, which is a high guard with the blade held vertically, appears only three times. If we lump both of these together, which for precision's sake, I *do not* recommend,[13] we get a posture that represents 13.8% of the given sample. Otherwise, the high guard appears only 12.5% of the time.

Other "standard" guards appear even less frequently. We find *ochs*[14] represented only ten times. In fact, other known postures do appear, but they are, with a single exception, in the "also ran" category. A "tail guard" (with the blade held behind the wielder, point away from the opponent like a tail) occurs only twice, representing only 0.8% of the depicted postures. One is, in fact, as likely to find the blade reversed, and used like a giant oversized dagger, as one is to find it under the left arm, and within the artwork, the blade as held over the left arm[15] appears no more often than the high guard. A right-side forward position does occur fairly often, but this raises its own question, as it is usually unclear, in an era not containing stop-motion photographic aesthetics within its art, whether such a position represents a guard, or else is depicting an active thrust. One curiosity is the aforementioned Beinecke MS229. In this Arthurian manuscript, figures in the marginalia are found with sword and buckler, and some of the postures they use are represented in Royal Armouries MS I.33[16] as well—however, with the exception of the high guard, none of these positions are *ever* shown being used by any of the knightly combatants. This is an interesting and exceptional case, which would require specialist expertise to address, as a brief image survey such as mandated in this study cannot determine the relevance of the marginalia to the primary text. Because this manuscript requires special care, it has not been directly included into the representational analysis.

The single posture for which we have any Fechtbuch reference, which also makes it into the top six, i.e., ten occurrences or greater in medieval art, is, in fact, the very most common posture of all. That, probably to the delight of students of I.33, is a depiction of the blade held upright at the shoulder. The "Priest's Special Second Guard," or the so-called "Walpurgis" guard, occurs with some variations no less than 42 times, nearly 20% of the total sample.[17] If nothing else, this certainly helps to lend credibility to I.33 as representing "fencing in earnest" – unlike so many of the other positions in our fencing manuscripts which we would expect to see used both in play and at war but appear only rarely in the latter, this posture is commonly depicted in a combat context.

In all, we have: Walpurgis, 18.8%; rear with point forward, 15.6%; 12.5% each for rear with vertical point and for some variation of "overhead"; 11.2% placed to the side and point up; and 8.9% for a very extended version of "to the rear, point forward," which itself could plausibly be considered a simple variation. In other words, even if we remove the high guard or "overhead" stance, 67% of the images shown depict fighters in stances one will generally not see in any of the later Fechtbücher.[18] No "iron door," no "boar" to speak of, almost no *ochs*,[19] a nearly non-existent *turret*[20] and *nebenhut*,[21] and not a single *posta di donna*.[22]

The results from contemporary and later, purely Western European sources are just as dramatic. The well-known image of footmen fighting in the Holkham Picture Bible, c. 1327–1335[23] depicts high guard twice, the over-arm posture once, and one depiction of an unusual cross-body posture, which I have not found elsewhere.

The Morgan Bible has 36 depictions of high guard, 12 depictions of the Priest's Special Second Guard,[24] one instance of the *turret*, and eight postures that are close to, but not quite, ochs.[25] The *Life of Saint Edward the Confessor* shows the same pattern as the survey through Nicolle's work: ten instances of high guard, one of ochs (and two of the above-mentioned "proto-ochs"), one instance of the weapon held in the "rear vertical" position, and 5 in the "Rear Point-Forward" posture. The *Grandes Chronique de France* is a bit of an outlier, with ochs depicted 8 times, high guard 3 times, and one instance apiece of a low horizontal position (possibly depicting the beginning of a thrust), and one with the blade in a dagger-like position pointing down.

The illustrations in manuscripts of Froissart's *Chronicles* continue the pattern. Taking all four manuscripts together (the first, Bibliothèque National FN 2643, having as many relevant images as the other three combined), we see high guard depicted 86 times, ochs 16 times, a position with the blade like ochs but slightly angled off to the side 11 times, rear-vertical 3 times, low-and-horizontal 4 times, and held for a two-handed thrust twice. In addition, one instance occurs of a cross-body posture similar to that depicted within the fight of the footmen from the Holkham Picture Bible.

Frequency of Guards Found in Medieval Artwork

"Walpurgis" (Priest's Special Second)	18.8%
High Guard	(12.5%)
Rear, Point Forward	15.6%
Rear, Point Vertical	12.5%
Side and Vertical	11.2%
Extended Rear	8.9%

Under Left Arm	0.8%
Over Left Arm	1.3%
Reversed Blade	0.8%
Ochs	4.5%
"True" High guard	1.3%
Down	0.4%
Tail	0.8%
Right side and forward (methodologically dangerous)	2.7–10.2%

For some reason, like the preliminary survey, the vast majority of the fighting postures known from the "Fechtbuch era" are simply absent within these manuscripts. But facts are stubborn things, and a literal approach to the art of the sword demonstrates quite clearly that the Fechtbuch material is clearly *not* being well-represented in the artistic products which were made primarily for the consumption of the social class most closely connected to swordplay. Rather than there being "one" art of the sword, at this point swordplay appears to be depicted quite differently depending on the context the artist is portraying: put bluntly, images of warfare don't seem to show the same fighting postures as are shown in images from the context of practice and training.

Let us proceed to the metaphorical level on which most of us are operating when we discuss the "art of the sword." To resume the discussion of guards, let us discuss longpoint (a posture in which the sword is held with the point outstretched, as if after a thrust). It is understandable why longpoint would gather attention; after all, the thrust is important, and many schools of fencing use and threaten a thrust. However, a look at the artwork being shown distinguishes the posture readily from that of other systems in which the point is extended.

Not many styles of fencing, medieval, modern, or otherwise, advocate a position that is square to the opponent, forward-weighted, leaning forward with the torso, and have not one, but *both* arms completely extended. At this point, the only way one could conclude that there was anything universal about the longpoint as expressed in I.33 is to begin to *explain away*, rather than explain, the use of the guard. That's because, as any boxer, fencer, golfer, or busboy can tell you, how you balance your body in relation to other objects matters. The entire system in I.33 is predicated on a "right down the middle" body stance that is extremely unusual in western literature and sport, and is entirely missing from other medieval and renaissance swordsmanship treatises.

So perhaps the continuity isn't to be found in issues of stance. How about in basic actions and fighting principles?

> *Note that the entire heart of the art of combat lies in this final guard, which is called Longpoint, and all actions of the guards or of the sword finish or have their conclusion in this one, and not in others....*
>
> *And when you close with him thinking that you have the correct measure and believe that you can reach him, and then you shall go at him quickly and with speed to the head and to the body. You will hit or miss and win the first strike, and not let him come to anything as you will hear hereafter in the true teaching....*
>
> *You do what you should when you bravely rush the opponent with the first strike as you will know hereafter....*
>
> *Be quick and steady without faltering, at once so that he cannot strike....*[26]

Tactically, the so-called "German school"—and I use the qualifier there on purpose—is miles apart from what Fiore dei Liberi teaches. The anonymous author of GNM 3227a, the earliest record of the teachings of the German ur-master Johannes Liechtenaeuer, essentially says, "hit him, then hit him again, and again and again. Have a plan and execute it, and you'll be safe because your opponent will never be able to get the initiative." This is the *core teaching* of what we call "Liechtenaeuerian swordplay." The manuscript's author reinforces this consistently.

But what about the "master cuts"? The Liechtenaeuerian tradition shows specific strikes that "break"[27] other guard positions or actions, and thus are often misconstrued purely as counterattacks. We see neophytes all over the historical fencing community using these *Meisterhauen* to play a counter-punching game, where the poor attacker is lured into attacking, generally with an *oberhau* (a strike from above, usually from the right side), at which point the defender counters with a *zwerchhau* (a horizontal strike that turns the blade over, thus closing the line of the attacker's cut while threatening a counter-cut) and finishes the strike by thrusting at the attacker in Ochs, the defender's horizontal blade keeping the attacker's weapon safely away from the line of engagement where it can do any good. But the author of 3227a doesn't care about that, and tells you how to counter these sorts of defenses. Against an unskilled opponent or a buffalo, you just hit him.

Against a master, he advises possibly the single-most-neglected line of text in the entire Liechtenaeuerian tradition: "Strike crooked to the flat of the master when you wish to weaken him."[28] We do not see this in I.33, or Marozzo, or Fiore, or Silver, for that matter. You *will* find it in Leckuchner and other fencers of Liechtenaeuer's tradition, on the other hand. It's a matter of feel, or *fühlen*.[29] If your opponent is weak when you go to hit him, great! Continue and hit him. But if he's strong, your blow will be finished. MS3227a says that you should attack with a strike at the upper openings, and preferably over your opponent's hilt.[30] It sounds like a fool's game to attack into such a solidly-defended position, thus resulting in the strike-counterpunch so commonly seen among those reconstructing this work. But the crooked strike, as MS 3227a states, *breaks* (defeats) the ochs. So in actuality, the author of 3227a isn't advocating suicide—far from it. He's advocating for the attacker to strike at a region where a skilled opponent's response will generally be predictable (either a zwerchau or an opposing oberhau[31]) because his other responses are for the most part, coffin-bait. By launching the first attack, you thereby control the response and can immediately remain strong on the sword and in possession of the initiative, forcing your opponent into *Nach*[32] and keeping him there until you're done with him. The advice given is worth quoting in full.

> *And when you must fight for your neck [i.e. for your life], then you shall use the earlier described teachings and seek and win the first strike with a good cross strike. When you go against another, then as soon as you think that you can reach him, with a step or leap, explode with a cross strike from high on the right side using the back edge straight at the head. And you shall let the point shoot out and move across well so that you drive the point well and turn or tightens it around the opponent's head like a belt. So that when you do a cross strike with a good step or leap out to the side, it is impossible for the opponent to protect himself or turn away. And when you thus win the first strike with the cross strike at one side, then regardless if you hit or miss, you shall at once and without delay win the after strike with the cross strike to the other side using the forward edge before the other can collect himself and come to blows or other techniques according to the afore described teachings. And you shall cross strike to both sides, to the ox and to the plough that is to the upper and the lower opening, from one side to the other, above and below continuously and without any interruptions so that you are in constant motion and the opponent can not come to blows. And each time that you do a cross strike above or below, then you do it well and throw the sword across above, well in front of your head so that you are well covered.*[33]

That's quite a bit different from what Fiore has to say. Here's how Fiore approaches the guards.[34]

> *And these are called poste, or guards, or the First Masters of the Duel. And they wear a crown on their head because they are placed in a position and in a way apt to make a grand defense, in this waiting.*
>
> *And Posta means the way of waiting for your enemy and offending him, without danger for yourself. . . .*
>
> *I wait for you without moving in Porta di Ferro, ready to grapple with all of my skill. . . .*
>
> *This play is called colpi di villano, and is made in this way. That is, you have to wait for the villano to strike with his sword. . . .*
>
> *I am the Position of the True Cross, because with a cross I defend myself and all the art of fencing and armed combat defends itself with covers of the crossed-weapon armed combat. Attack, because I am waiting for you well. . . .*
>
> *I am the noble Position of the Window on the Right, which in beating-back and injuring I am always ready, and a long spear bothers me little. Also with the sword I could wait for the long spear, standing in this guard which beats-back all thrusts, and retards them. . . .*

Does this mean that Fiore never advocates throwing the first strike? No. But his style is fundamentally that of a fencer who prefers to parry and then riposte: he's waiting for his opponent to define the tactical space by "putting something out there," and then reacting in such a manner that he escapes injury while hurting the other guy. Perhaps the best example of this, commonly seen in his system, is the exchange of thrusts, a tactic that survives to this day in boxing as the "cross," which originally didn't simply mean "right hand punch," but rather a punch which crossed over and subtly displaced an incoming punch in precisely the same way that Fiore's exchange of thrusts does with the longsword. The exchange of thrusts, on the other hand, is completely missing from the Liechtenaeuer tradition: it's not a play that makes sense in a system built around seizing the initiative from the moment one is in range to strike. There may be additional reasons for this sort of differentiation, such as duels where the duty to strike first or to wait for a strike was socially constrained, or in instances of urban self-defense where there was some legal reason why one did not wish to be recognized as the aggressor.

Even inside the so-called "German school," though, one finds differences. After the insistence on seizing the *Vor*, one of the most important principles from Liechtenaeuer is to work *am schwert* with windings, using *fühlen* to manipulate the geometry of the fight so that one can continue pounding on the opponent until something gets through. But that tactic isn't universally obeyed by Liechtenaeuer's successors, either.

My second-favorite Talhoffer[35] plate of all time demonstrates quite clearly that he's advertising his wares. His advertisement addresses that tactical situation all martial arts instructors know and love—that of the opponent who makes one attack and then stands stock-still while the defender performs an impressive and lethal, but also complicated, maneuver.[36] Specifically, in this plate, Talhoffer deflects a cut from above by cutting upwards into the attack. The then steps forward to trap the blade under his arm while simultaneously thrusting into him with his own weapon. There may not be perfect continuity in medieval fencing methods, but it's quite clear that continuity in six centuries of martial-arts *advertising* remains solid. There are more counters to this than you can shake a spear at. But we'll get to the English in a minute.

Notice something: Talhoffer is advocating what in modern fencing terms is called an "expulsion," which will then be used as an opportunity to trap the blade. You see this fairly regularly in Fiore's work and elsewhere, but it's about as far from *fühlen am schwert* as you can possibly get,[37] and is quite a bit different than the majority of Leckuchner's fencing with the single-handed messer, which not only *does* advocate the fight *am schwert,* but goes into excruciating levels of detail about where the various plays can wind up.

It's not just Talhoffer, either. The same position shown there is called the "double-shield," and the same expulsion is advocated by none other than Ringeck himself, in his Dresden codex glossa:

> *Then, from the stroke from below: if he strikes at you from above from his right shoulder, wind against him to your left side against your shield, so that you stand in the "double shield." Then wind openly to your right side and attack his face. If he defends against it and holds his shield high, take the left leg. This can be done on both sides.*[38]

It's not just sword and buckler, either—we see it in the Codex Wallerstein:

> *Next one strikes downwards at your head, so deflect with your flat and on your crosspiece, and push his falchion to the side, so that he has to strike. And when he wants to strike, find the openings and chop his arm off. ...*[39]

Not only does the Codex Wallerstein advocate an expulsion, it's also suggesting that the fencer wait for his opponent's action, rather than remaining in the Vor and completing the action with a thrust or pommel strike, or simply passing through and striking at the upper openings, a technique which ought to succeed whether the opponent tries to convert to either a blow or a thrust. Notice that while it may not always be *possible* to keep the initiative and thus "remain in the Vor," this is a case of the author expressly advocating that the opponent not even try to do so. Such advice is diametrically opposed to the logic discussed above which is espoused in GNM 3227a.

If not all German fencing manuscripts seem to have been predicated upon using *fühlen am schwert,* thus rendering it "optional" for the so-called "German" or "Liechtenaeuer" School, we can conclude reasonably well that it was entirely unknown in England, at least given the extant manuscript evidence. Consider George Silver's late sixteenth-century defense of good, proper English fencing:

> *The second cause is, the lack of the knowledge in due observance of the four actions, the which we shall call bent, spent, lying spent, and drawing back. These actions every man fights upon, whether they are skillful or unskillful. . . .*[40]

The four actions described by Silver are: Bent (when one is prepared to strike), Spent (when one's strike has been thrown), Lying Spent (when one's strike has been thrown but before one has recovered sufficiently to throw another one), and Drawing Back (the period in which one prepares to throw another strike, thus leading directly to "Bent," and completing the cycle). Generally speaking, there's nothing wrong with Silver's four actions. They don't seem to be particularly controversial, and neither am I aware of them being addressed at length even by partisans of Italianate swordplay who disagree with Silver regarding the rapier. But they're important: if these are the four actions of the fight, it's no surprise that Silver disdains Italianate and Spanish fencing: Silver's system does not acknowledge the stringing of the blades[41] or *fühlen am schwert.* We can tell this because if one is fighting according to such a system, the third of Silver's four actions, that of "lying spent," literally doesn't exist! In this sense, those who characterized English fencing as akin to chopping wood may have had a point: the system is predicated upon the idea that one must retract one's weapon prior to launching another attack—something that is about as far from the Continental swordplay of the era as it is possible to get. Those who study Silver closely may recall that his "Governors" advise: "if at first you don't succeed—*fly out* in order to try, try again."[42] This is completely consistent with what little we know of English Longsword from the fifteenth century. Neither the Ledall[43] or Cotton Titus[44] Manuscript even mention blade-to-blade contact, let alone *fühlen am schwert.* The Harleian Manuscript[45] mentions it in the context of practicing with and without blade contact, but without any context which would shed additional light on the problem.[46] All three, however, emphasize "voiding" (avoiding) enemy blows. Based on the evidence at hand, we can say that there appears to be a distinct regional difference between fencing as taught in England and in the Holy Roman Empire.

So if tactics and fighting principles don't satisfy our quest for the One True Art of the Sword, what about addressing the issue on a higher level, as an allegorical or topological statement for the swordsman himself and his diligence and training in moving, exploiting openings, etc.? Well, here too, the idea breaks down. Training is conditioning, as any sports coach will tell you, and different training results in *different conditioning.*[47] That's why cross-training is so popular for athletes who are stuck in a rut.

Numerous fencing manuscripts of the period[48] show movement principles which are present in some of the other fencing styles, but absent in others. Boar's Tooth aptly illustrates the "hands and toes, same side goes" body movement style characterized in Fiore's work. In Fiore's work, one never sees the torso twist—if one steps forwards into Boar's Tooth, the same arm, leg, and side move forward. The arms are thus never forced to cross the centerline, where the presence of a rigid breastplate could hinder one's movements, nor step forward with one side of the body while twisting forward with the other, which could cause binding problems in the case of an ill-tailored mail shirt combined with rigid armor. The shoulders and hips rotate together, and are never depicted in counter-rotation. While making for a style that's not exceptionally fluid, it *does* make perfect sense for a style which is intended to do double duty for when one is unarmored, or wearing rigid and restrictive harness.

Moving like this also allows for extremely fine control of distance, to the point where one can almost feel a bout seem to "slow down," because one is able to move one's body in a way that makes the speed of a sword strike seem trivial. While it *sounds* like a simple thing, developing true mobility in such a style takes practice and can be utterly exhausting. Anyone who doubts this can test the hypothesis easily by taking a walk to their local store some time without ever allowing their hips and shoulders to counter-rotate.

This is starkly different than I.33, where the upper torso must be able to alter its shape dramatically while counter-rotating through the hips. The so-called "Walpurgis" guard, for instance, places the hand alongside the chest, relatively near the armpit.[49] To cut effectively from this position requires significant explosiveness and suppleness in the shoulder and quite possibly the rib cage as well. In the Plow the buckler hand is held extended while the weapon is extended. But here we see that the forearm is rotated so that the palm actually faces outwards. This is consistent with the slope of the arm as depicted in the image, and while highly counter-intuitive and requiring some flexibility, it also have significant advantages. By locking the bones of the forearm together (as happens when the hand is turned outward), the elbow and shoulder directly support the weight of the arm and sword, making it much less difficult to maintain this position for a given length of time than would be the case were the hand in another position. Additionally, directly supported by the shoulder, the fencer is "grounded"[50] to receive an impact while skewering an opponent. Effective fighting in this method presupposes significant shoulder flexibility, not to mention sufficiently strong calves and ankles that numerous modern re-enactors have dismissed the footwork positions entirely, insisting that they are impossible and represent mere stylistic artwork.

Similarly, Leckuchner's messer fencing shows actions requiring great arm flexibility (simply striking effectively from its high vertical "turret" guard described earlier in this paper requires very supple shoulders, for instance), just like I.33, but also frequently shows explosive footwork movements predicated upon very good hip flexibility which would be utterly impractical in heavy armor. Figures routinely crouch low into stances which would require significant hip strength to enter and exit fluidly, or else take long strides with relatively straight legs. Neither of these would be practical while wearing heavy armor. And, of course, if one wants to see an example of style which is utterly predicated upon the conditioning of the legs for strength and the hips for turnout at a level to make young ballerinas wince, one need only to look at Meyer's later sporting method, where the thrust was disallowed and low stances therefore gave a significant advantage on both offense and defense. In Meyer's work it is quite common to see fencers fighting with long, low, open stances with the thighs nearly horizontal and feet often facing in opposite directions. This is significantly more demanding on the legs and hips than the postures of modern fencing, postures which we know require significant conditioning if the athlete is going to be able to move effectively.

Diligent practice of any one of these schools of fighting will result in a combatant or athlete (of course, the two not being entirely distinguishable) who has a markedly different body and way of moving than the other, and which will give one movement habits that can make it difficult to cross-train in other schools.

These movement habits, once long-habituated, are ingrained at a level beneath the conscious mind, and many students literally don't know what they're doing with their bodies, only that they find some movements "natural," and others "dangerous and unnatural." I regularly encountered this myself as a savateur training Muay Thai students who moved much like Fiore's style advocates, and who were unused to generating power with twists of the torso. I later found out that one of these students thought adapting to savate was really difficult, but what really blew his mind was all those "freaky people" who could *actually play golf.* The oft-misused dictum among martial artists that "there are only so many ways a body can move" reveals much more about the martial artist saying it than about the human body's actual potential.

In conclusion, if there's a true art to the sword, we don't see it in artwork. It's not reflected in fighting postures. It doesn't show up in tactics or fighting principles, and it's absolutely not found in our interpretations of how different schools of swordsmanship move. Perhaps, finally, we have to turn to the realm of ideas, and an anagogical frame of reference. It would certainly be reasonable and within bounds to say that there is an *idea* of fencing that encompasses everything I've discussed so far, found in the underlying ultimate reality that all of these individuals accepted. Now, whether such an idea was *actually* real, or a psychological tool which was more or less nominal, is something I'd hesitate to venture an opinion on. I'd especially hesitate to venture such an opinion during the period when many of these texts were written, particularly if I were to myself suddenly within the confines of the Universities of Prague or Paris.

Either way, this approach to ideas is one that the vast majority of these authors took for granted; many of them were, after all, well-educated priests, or else, like Fiore dei Liberi, were connected to some of the highest courts of the land. Not only were they familiar with these frames of reference, they were *expected* to be familiar with them, and to use them. In essence, the idea that there is "one true art of the sword" is not something which should be taken by those trying to "bring life to these bones" as having any material or literal validity whatsoever. Much like the absolute *mania* over symbol books and allegory which overtook European intellectuals by the time some of these later references were being written, the statement is a way of saying that one speaks the language, knows the code, *gets it.* Somewhat like the fairly awful way I've structured this entire article as a sort of horrid pun on the so-called "medieval four-fold method of exegesis" (my apologies to any scriptural specialists reading this article).

We are dealing here not with anything that is true on any technical level, but which is, quite frankly, "boilerplate" language used in order to establish that one is worth being paid attention to, rather than just some ignoramus with a piece of steel. And we *should* pay attention to them. But we should also remember that the writers of this time were embedded in a social and cultural context just like we are, and not let ourselves get too carried away with ideas that sound great in the abstract, but which turn out to be nonsense once the peel is off the orange.

Endnotes

1. For convenience and because of this article's specific focus on swordplay (rather than, for instance, wrestling or dagger work), I am using this term interchangeably with *Fechtbuch*, "martial arts manual," et cetera.
2. This can be defined in many ways, depending on the martial arts or fencing style. In this case, I refer to a straight line between the fencer and his opponent, and whether that line goes directly in front of the fencer, perpendicular to the body or breastbone, or else emerges at an angle, creating a "center line" which places one side of the opponent's body closer to the opponent than the other side.
3. David Nicolle, *Arms and Armour of the Crusading Era 1050–1350: Western Europe and the Crusader States,* vol. 1 (London: Greenhill Books, 1999). The material in the second volume is less relevant to the study, involving images from as far away as India and Japan.
4. Insofar as the depiction of heterogeneous methods constituted an *actual* problem. The fundamental issue was actually that my thesis was predicated upon looking for a universal pattern which turned out not to exist.
5. Yale Beinecke Library MS 229
6. Pierpont Morgan Library, MS M.638, also known as the Maciejowski Bible
7. Cambridge University Library MS Ee.3.59
8. British Library Additional MS 47682
9. Bibliothèque Nationale MS Français 2813
10. Bibliothèque Nationale MS Français 2643–2646, respectively. No particularly notable regionalisms were apparent within the artwork.
11. Indeed, *many* martial arts use postures which do not initially appear to make sense to an outsider. It would be unusual if this were not also occasionally the case with medieval martial arts as well.
12. The "turret" is a posture which is similar to the more common *vom tag* insofar as it has the sword held overhead. What distinguishes it from the more general posture, however, is that the weapon is held vertically. While the difference may sound minor, holding the blade in a true vertical, rather than merely overhead, requires the muscles of the back, shoulder, and arm to work differently, with the result that actions which are easy to perform from one are more difficult from the other, and vice versa.
13. Because there are significant differences in actually fencing from these two postures, even though the difference may seem trivial to a non-fencer
14. A fencing posture which which holds the sword horizontally, with the hilt somewhere near the head, and the point outstretched towards the opponent. The *ochs* is a *very* common "bread-and-butter" guard throughout the German fencing manuscript traditions, and one which has parallels throughout the Italian literature as well.
15. First and Third Wards, respectively
16. One of the earliest surviving fencing manuscripts, which depicts the use of single-handed sword and buckler. For a dedicated student of sword and buckler, therefore, Beinecke MS 229 is thus of great importance.
17. These variations are fairly trivial considering the number of sources represented: blade slightly backwards vs. perfectly vertical, and some minor variation in the hand height.
18. The aforementioned problems of realism apply, of course. But since these works were commissioned for an audience which was highly-trained in the use of arms, one may assume at basic level of realism (and in the author's opinion, often a highly-sophisticated level of realism) regarding how the warriors are shown moving.
19. A high guard with the sword held horizontally, point facing the opponent, it is common in German manuscripts.
20. A high guard primarily found in messer fencing, with the blade held high and in a true vertical rather than being slanted to the front, back, or side.

21. A *nebenhut*, or "tail guard," points the sword to the rear, hilt facing the opponent. This seemingly counter-intuitive posture threatens a cut while removing the sword arm as a viable target. It is a guard which appears occasionally in the Liechtenaeuer tradition.
22. A special high guard in which the sword is hung over the rear shoulder, with the opposite flank turned towards the opponent as if to threaten a powerful cut. It does this, but also threatens a powerful direct thrust.
23. British Library MS 47682, 42v
24. Within a common variation: all instances show the blade tilted backwards.
25. The general body posture is equivalent, but consistently held further back than a true *ochs*.
26. Nürnberger Handschrift MS 3227a, 16r, 16v, 17, 25r, 28r.
27. The term "breaking" is used in a manner synonymous with "countering."
28. GNM 3227a, 25r
29. In this style of swordplay, one generally "feels" for the point of leverage between the two weapons, flowing with it rather than seeking to oppose force with force.
30. GNM 3227a, 16r
31. An *oberhau* is simply an attack coming from above, whereas a *zwerchau* is an oberhau which elevates the sword hilt while turning over to strike the opponent with its "false" edge.
32. While this can mean simply "after" the opponent, in this case it refers to a situation where the opponent possesses the initiative and is thus able to strongly influence what one can and cannot do.
33. MS3227a, 28r. I am using Jeffrey Hull's translation here, available online at: http://wiktenauer.com/wiki/Codex_D%C3%B6bringer_(MS_3227a), accessed March 19, 2013.
34. MS Ludwig XV 13, quotations from 2r, 2r, 8r-c, 14–c, 37v-b, 9r–c, respectively.
35. Hans Talhoffer was a fifteenth-century fencing master who taught in Swabia, and is considered to be a follower of Liechtenaeuer. Talhoffer is credited with at least half a dozen different fencing manuscripts. See Mark Rector, *Medieval Combat: a Fifteenth-Century Illustrated Manual of Swordfighting and Close-Quarter Combat* (London: Greenhill Books, 2000), 9–19.
36. BSB Cod.icon.39ra Schwaben 1467 119v, 120r.
37. It's important for fencers with modern training to remember that in spite of its surface appearance, *fuhlen am schwert* does not express the same idea as "sentiment du fer." Though expressions of the idea do indeed differ among different teachers, the latter generally refers to the ability to gain tactile feedback through one's weapon, which is also implied by the larger idea expressed by *fuhlen am schwert*. However, the medieval idea adds a predicate meaning, where one not only feels one's opponent's actions, but instantly matches one's level of force to contrast that offered by the opponent. This is fundamentally alien to much of modern fencing, including nearly the entirety of modern sabre fencing.
38. MS Dresden C487, 54v
39. Universitätsbibliothek Augsburg Codex I.6.4°.2, 31r
40. George Silver. *Paradoxes of Defence* (London, 1599.), 5
41. The term "stringing" derives from "stringere," which in Italian has several meanings, but is best translated in English as "tightening in" or "narrowing." In fencing, it refers to actions on the blade when one is consciously attempting to maintain blade contact with one's opponent.
42. This is a comparison which stretches out to Elizabethan England, and therefore is somewhat suspect. Unfortunately, the contemporary English longsword manuscript only describes solo practice, and therefore cannot address the questions being asked in this paper.
43. British Library Additional MS 39564
44. British Library Cotton MS Titus A.xxv, folio 105 (r/v)
45. British Library Harleian Manuscript 3542
46. Since it at least mentions swords touching, unlike the other two, it's possible that additional material shedding light on its meaning would force a reappraisal of English fencing of the time.

47. Using muscles in different patterns places different stresses on the body, and there is no such thing as "universal" conditioning, which would prepare one to do any sport equally well. For instance, cyclists and marathoners are both endurance athletes, and each athlete would have a considerable advantage in endurance over a sedentary person, but endurance, aerobic or otherwise, in the former sport does not provide similar performance in the latter. This is one reason why it is very unusual to find a professional athlete who can excel in more than one field, and why martial artists who excel in one style can find even the basic techniques of a different style to be exhausting to perform.
48. See Royal Armouries MS I.33 14Eiii, No.20, D, vi, f 19r and 7v respectively; Pissani-Dossi MS carta 4a; Joachim Meyers Faktbok MS A.4°.2, Lunds Universitets Bibliotek, p. 7; CGM 582 (1482), 62v.
49. How near would be an interpretive issue for specialists, again touching on the "realism" debate.
50. "Grounded" refers to an alignment of the body where force is absorbed by the skeleton, requiring minimal muscular strength to either maintain a position, particularly in the face of opposing force.

"FORWARD INTO THE PAST": RE-ENACTORS AND THE QUEST FOR AUTHENTICITY

Lisa Evans

Five years ago, a remarkable piece of theater was staged in France. One of the earliest operas ever written, Stefano Landi's 1632 *dramma musicale Il Sant'Alessio,* was performed for the first time in almost three centuries. Not only that, the production was as close to what a seventeenth century audience would have seen as surviving records and modern research would allow.[1] Early music specialist William Christie and Les Artes Florissant, drawing on over thirty years of research into Baroque music and performance techniques,[2] had not only gone to great lengths to ensure that the costumes, sets, dance interludes, stage movement, and instruments were as authentic to the early seventeenth century as possible, but had even lit the entire production with candles, torches, and lanterns. The only inauthentic touch was, ironically enough, the singers themselves. Since the opera had originally been staged for high-ranking cardinals, many of the parts, including the lead, had been written for castrati. This forced Christie to substitute countertenors and boy trebles in the high voice parts to approximate the sound of the original all-male cast since there are, of course, no modern castrati.[3]

Despite, or perhaps because of, this painstaking research, *Il Sant'Alessio* was both musically satisfying and dramatically compelling as it told the story of an early Christian saint. Christie has long maintained that "historical knowledge should inform modern performance, not ossify it,"[4] and one need look no further than this production to see the truth of his words. Not only that, the use of authentic instruments, countertenors instead of female sopranos and mezzos, and authentic lighting yielded unexpected insights into past operatic conventions; the male singers in women's parts looked convincingly female in the warm glow of candlelight, and the clean vocal timbre of the falsettists and trebles gave the musical lines an otherworldly character that would not have been possible with the richer voices of women. The production was a fine example of what research, education, and dedication can do to create a sense of being in an earlier and very different time period.

It is not only professionals who engage in such efforts, however. Amateurs seeking to create the same sort of authentic experience for themselves and their audience seem to be everywhere: "Western martial artists" gathering in Poland to don medieval plate armor and duel with steel swords in "The Battle of the Nations," Civil War "soldiers" tromping about battlefields or impersonating the dead, World War II enthusiasts wearing actual Allied or Nazi uniforms as they drive about in Sherman tanks to recreate the Battle of the Bulge, and volunteers at a historic village interpreting old crafts for visitors by using the same tools, materials, and skills as in olden times.[5] Whether they're called re-enactors, living historians, or re-creationists, these men and women are part of a fast-growing, often misunderstood group:[6] History enthusiasts who not only study the past, but attempt on some level to bring it back to life in the twenty-first century.

Such immersion in the minutiae of the past is usually regarded as nothing more than a type of historical escapism, and at least in some cases, such an assumption would be correct.[7] Some re-enactors, however, are determined to take their hobby beyond dressing in funny clothes on the weekends. Their goal is nothing less than finding "the real answers, [reading] between the lines in the history books, and then [sharing their] experience with spectators."[8] This quest for being as authentic as possible in their evocation of a specific time and place can range from the practical (testing a possible method for weaving a ruffle-edged veil by varying warp tension and selvedge length on one's own loom)[9] to the absurd (discarding Granny Smith apples as "not period" during a Civil War march),[10] but at its best, the impulse that drives those who seek to recreate the past to delve so deeply into past forms and means of production results in a sort of experimental archaeology that can lead to genuine contributions to scholarship.

Arguably the most widely consumed and recognizable type of popular history,[11] re-enactment can encompass everything from a volunteer putting on a commercially made dress to lead tours at a local historical society to serious collectors assembling an entire kit of elaborate, expensive, and meticulously researched clothing or armor, assuming another name, and taking on another identity. Fortunately for the historically-minded, faithfulness to past forms and techniques has increased greatly over the last twenty years,[12] but there is still so much variation that it is best to begin by discussing the various types of re-enactment and re-enactors that have sprung up across the industrialized world.

Historian Jonathan Lamb has identified four distinct types of re-enactment: house (focused on the intimate details of history); pageant (large public commemorations specifically intended to instill a sense of community, such as the re-creation of historic events); theater (less serious public events intended to entertain, not inspire); and "real" (extreme realism, such as a Confederate infantryman who can, and does, convincingly imitate a bloated corpse on the battlefield).[13] Theater scholar Michael Cramer of the City University of New York, focusing more directly on participants than events, has gone further and identified three distinct sub-divisions within the larger community: re-enactors, such as Civil War buffs, who attempt to recreate specific events as accurately as possible; living historians, such as the British Ermine Street Guard, who seek to recreate an era and an ambience, sometimes as interpreters at historic sites; and re-creationists, such as members of the Society for Creative Anachronism (SCA), who take aspects of a time period and meld them with non-historical details to create something that may feel or look period but is actually a sort of performance art.[14]

For the purposes of this discussion, I will refer to all of these groups as re-enactors, for regardless of their level of authenticity, all strive on some level to bring a past era to life, and as such are crucial to the creation and preservation of the public memory of history.[15] For all that curators and archaeologists may rightly focus on the preservation, documentation, and restoration of the items and stories in their custody, their expertise may or may not extend to how these objects were used in their time. It therefore falls to others to make replicas of the material culture of the past in an attempt to rediscover once common practices that were never written down. Artifacts housed in museums may offer clues as to the lives and stories of their original owners,[16] but no matter how well conserved, an old cuirass or distaff is nothing more than an inert object until someone actually picks it up and attempts to use it. Sometimes it is only by donning the armor or spinning a thread that we can understand why the straps are positioned at a certain angle, or why so many old woodcuts show women cooking and tending their children with a distaff stuck in their girdles.

Some museums have taken advantage of re-enactors' specialization in material culture as part of their interpretative programs. Most often this takes the form of special events such as battle commemorations, but sometimes it may include re-enactors, either volunteers or paid professionals, as regular docents or demonstrators.[17] At the same time, the last decade has seen an increasing infiltration of material culture fields such as costume, textiles, cookery, and combat techniques by past and present members of the medieval re-creationist Society for Creative Anachronism and related groups who have written scholarly papers that draw at least partially on their experience in the living archaeology of re-enactment.[18]

Despite what would seem to be a logical partnership, it cannot be said that that the relationship between re-enactors and professionals is either completely smooth or particularly amiable. Amateurs may collect and recreate artifacts down to the adze marks, but trained historians point out that such an obsession with the concrete may result in the trivialization of the social and cultural matrix that produced the individual objects.[19] Although an "enthusiastic amateur can sometimes shed so much more light than an academic and professional,"[20] the non-professional is always at risk of falling victim to a sort of "arrogance of the amateur," as untrained enthusiasts who don't know nearly as much as they think they do either misinform the public or belittle the professionals.[21] Worse, not all re-enactors are suited to the role of scholar due to lack of training or public educator due to temperament or physical type,[22] while period-specific groups with high authenticity standards might have no place for members of certain ethnic groups, women, or non-combatants.[23] Since museums and living history sites must appeal to the public as a whole, an otherwise laudable concern with authenticity could interfere with the mandate to give a voice to all groups, whether documented or absent from the written record.[24]

There is also the question of motive. Re-enactors and professionals may share a love of history and a desire to interpret and preserve the past, but there is considerable intellectual and emotional distance between portraying a time period and attempting to provide a nuanced account of the social, economic, and cultural forces that made the pretty clothes and colorful artifacts possible. Professionals are right to point out that escapism is certainly a major impetus for some re-enactors, either out of a desire to experience a less complicated way of life or to gain a sense of personal empowerment and control that is lacking in so many aspects of modern existence.[25] At the same time, re-enactors are equally correct when they claim that a degree in history is not especially practical when attempting to understand why certain materials were used in in one context or culture and not another.[26]

One might assume that a shared love of history might serve as a bridge between the amateur and the professional. However, it is possible to study and reconstruct historic needlework without spending uncounted hours stitching a brand-new Elizabethan sweet bag,[27] and equally possible to wear a Roman legionnaire's kit on the weekends that is correct down to the oak-tanned leather without setting up a tannery in one's back yard. Why do some re-enactors take their hobby one step further by actually creating artifacts from start to finish?

The answer is deceptively simple: to learn what one's chosen time period was *really* like on the most basic level, either in terms of personal experience or material culture. This may mean translating neglected manuscripts and related documents to gain a sense of how early modern ecclesiastical textiles were cleaned,[28] studying old paintings for costume details and weaving samples of specific items using only period methods until one achieves a result similar to that portrayed in the art,[29] or taking a hitherto obscure subject and formulating the descriptive terms, analysis of surviving items, and assessment of materials used so that the next generation of researchers can build upon one's work in the future.[30]

Most commonly, however, it means engaging in experimental and experiential archaeology: researching a period example as thoroughly as possible, selecting what one believes are the best contemporary matches in terms of materials and tools, and creating, to the best of one's ability, a modern example of a period work. There are a few books and papers aimed at these researchers, especially in the field of costume studies, but this a recent development; it was not until the publication of the last, posthumous volume of Janet Arnold's *Patterns of Fashion* series that the publishers included detailed instructions on how to recreate some of the clothing and dress accessories studied in the book, despite the series' popularity among theater technicians and costume enthusiasts.[31] Most re-enactors have no choice but to engage in what one calls "back-engineering": studying original sources, some in unfamiliar languages; learning to make the right materials (or finding the equivalent); and only then making the desired artifact and sharing one's research with the larger community.[32]

My interview with a member of the SCA illustrates both the advantages and the disadvantages of this approach. R, as I will call her, is one of the few either in or out of the SCA who studies pre-modern quilting. She specializes in Welsh-style wholecloth linen trapunto and corded knotwork quilts, and hopes one day to "put together a collection of period designs [for publication]."[33] Her sources include period inventories containing references to old quilts, as well as modern books on wholecloth quilts, trapunto and other types of stuffed quilting, old Welsh quilts, and Celtic design.

R strives to use the closest materials possible to the linen fabric and cotton wadding used in period examples, although she is handicapped to a certain extent by the lack of access to suitable linen, cotton batting, and linen thread in Southern California.[34] At the time I spoke to her, she was working on a quilt in the style of the fourteenth-century Tristan quilt at the Victoria & Albert Museum in London and had devoted considerable time to studying recently released detail photographs taken by conservators who were engaged in stabilizing the quilt for restoration. In addition, she is one of the few people in her immediate area who still quilts by hand instead of machine, making her a sort of "living resource" for anyone wishing to study old quilting techniques, regardless of time period.

In many ways R's practical approach to her art is similar to that of textile researcher Carla Tilghman, who took great pains to use the same type and weight of linen used in period veils when she recreated Giovanna Cenami's veil from Jan van Eyck's *The Arnolfini Wedding.*[35] However, lack of access to books on quilt history as opposed to technique and design had led R to believe that Welsh wholecloth quilting, which can be documented only to the eighteenth century, was similar enough to earlier forms to be considered correct to period. She was in turn passing this logical but erroneous belief on to others, making her work, as skilled and decorative as it is, is a cautionary tale of amateur overreach and the dangers of extrapolating from limited sources.[36]

Not all re-enactors make such flawed assumptions, or are handicapped by lack of access to primary or secondary sources. In particular, groups based in areas blessed with readily accessible period sites, museums, and artifacts have a significant advantage over less geographically blessed groups: they can study the actual places and objects instead of relying on photographs or web sites.

This advantage is particularly evident in the work of British medieval and Dark Ages re-enactors. Unlike American medievalists, their members can visit the actual places where famous battles took place, easily contact local museums housing period artifacts and clothing, and see castles, Iron Age hill forts, and ancient hedgerows during their daily commutes. Standards are much higher than in American groups (including the European branch of the SCA),[37] to the point that that marriages have failed due to the time and money required to produce proper period shoes, clothing, and armor.[38] The legendary Ermine Street Guard, which specializes in early Roman Britain, is so devoted to maintaining its magnificent kit that they only demonstrate Roman tactical maneuvers, not fighting, for fear of damaging their armor and weapons—which belong to the Guard as a legal entity, not to the individual members.[39] It is little wonder that the Guard is regularly paid for the demo work at museums, castles, and historic sites, or that two somewhat later groups with strict historical standards, Regia Anglorum and Britannia, regularly appear in period films such as *Gladiator*.[40]

At the same time, the Guard's quest for the perfect armor, or sword, or hand-sewn goatskin tent, falls short of bringing the past to life because the armor, swords, and tents, are never actually used as intended. The insights that members have gained through their work and research lack the final element of knowing whether their re-creations would hold up in a real battle, or that their tent would actually protect them during inclement weather. For all their emphasis on looking exactly like the Roman soldiers who garrisoned ancient Briton, they do not and cannot know what it was like to *be* such a soldier because they do not engage in the most fundamental military activity: going on campaign and engaging an enemy. A SCA neophyte in plastic armor and a rattan sword who goes out and fights in a rainstorm may have a better sense of the mindset of an ancient soldier than these beautifully equipped Britons.[41] If R and her lack of proper books and materials represents one issue facing re-enactors, surely creating something so perfect that one dare not use it is equally problematic.

It must also be pointed out that, on some level, we already know that the methods used by artisans of three hundred years ago worked, even if we may not always know the exact technique; the objects they made are still here to be examined and admired and sometimes even used so whether or not a certain thing was possible is not at issue. Surely it must be possible to strike a happy medium between professional and amateur, or between enjoyment and perfection, to produce something that it simultaneously correct, educational, and entertaining for participants and spectators alike. Fortunately for all who love material culture, a recent collaboration between professionals and re-enactors is perhaps the best recent example of the potential benefits of such an alliance: the Plimoth Jacket Project.

The Project began in 2006 when needlework teacher and MIT alumna Tricia Wilson Nguyen was approached by the curatorial staff at Plimoth Plantation, a living history site that aims to recreate the early days of Puritan Massachusetts. The museum planned an exhibit on how the early colonists dressed themselves, centering on one of the elaborate embroidered jackets worn by wealthy upper class Englishwomen in the Jacobean period.[42]

These jackets, which were worked in rich silks, metallic lace, and tiny spangles, used stitches that were no longer taught, employed materials that were no longer made, and required the sort of precise, meticulous technique that is all but lost. Making a modern version would not only result in a garment, but would be a way to educate the public while, as Nguyen put it, "enabl[ing] the specialist communities to execute the embroidery and lace while sharing [the professionals'] expertise with them to build skills and join knowledge bases."[43] Although Nguyen does not use the word "re-enactor," her meaning was clear: with the possible exception of a few groups like the Embroiderers' Guild of America, the logical place to find modern Americans with the knowledge of early seventeenth century embroidery techniques was the re-enactment community.

This is exactly what the curatorial staff at Plimoth Plantation did. In addition to researching the cut and construction of surviving Jacobean jackets, the Project relied on time estimates worked out by re-enactor and interpreter Laura Mellin,[44] an Elizabethan specialist who embroidered a monochrome silk jacket based on two extant examples.[45] Mellin herself joined the estimated 250 individuals who actually worked on the embroidery, lace, and spangles over a three year period, and she was far from the only re-enactor involved; not only did several re-enactors work on the elaborate silk embroidery, Nguyen's business, Thistle Threads, sold kits teaching obscure stitches to potential stitchers, many of which ended up in the hands of SCA members who later worked on the embroidery.

Unfortunately for the Project, the planned exhibition on colonial dress had to be scrapped due to economic conditions. The Jacket itself, which was completed late in 2009, went on exhibit at Winterthur Museum in Delaware until a place could be found for it at Plimoth Plantation, and its eventual home is still not clear. However, its mere existence was a milestone in American needlework, and in many ways a fulfillment of the Project's original goals. Much was learned about the actual construction of these jackets, and that information was shared with the public. The gilt silk twist used to make the original jackets is now commercially available for the first time in centuries, along with instructions on how to execute the complex stitches of an earlier time. Knowledge that had been lost was reclaimed through the efforts of professional and re-enactor alike, and textile community as a whole is richer for the experience.

For re-enactors, living historians, or re-creationists, the desire to know what the past was *really* like is more than simple escapism. Re-enactment strives to further this despite inevitably reminding both participant and spectator of the essential *otherness* of the past, for its ultimate goal is to create a sense of the past as a whole and compete phenomenon, not the messy, fragmented experience that comprises actual life and actual history.[46] And for all the silliness that can ensue when, say, a "living historian" purports to talk about a non-existent "quilt code" used by runaway slaves,[47] the best reeanctors can and do engage in the sort of happy tunnel vision that leads to new insights about the material culture and mindset of the past that archival research cannot.

For all the stereotype of the living history/re-creationist/re-enactor community as a group of people escaping from the twentieth century, participants in these groups contribute to the larger historical community. Many lack formal training, but their willingness to engage in unpaid experimental archaeology, research old methods of production and long-lost folkways, and work outside the academic community for the sheer love of their art can yield promising results. "Amateur" in its simplest context means "lover of the work," and the love that inspires these amateurs, whether academically inclined or not, is ultimately what allows them to produce work that enriches the store of knowledge for everyone who studies the past.

Endnotes

1. Raymond Tuttle, "DVD Review: *Il Sant'Alessio*," on *Classical Net* http://www.classical.net/music/recs/reviews/v/vir89999dvdb.php, accessed April 12, 2012.
2. Nicholas Wroe, "A Life in Music: William Christie," *The Guardian*, June 19, 2009 http://www.guardian.co.uk/culture/2009/jun/20/william-christie-baroque-music-interview, accessed April 23, 2012.
3. Tuttle
4. Wroe
5. Jay Gaynor, "Why Do We Cast Cannons, Make Wooden Wheels, and Build Coffeehouses?" http://colonialwilliamsburg.org/Foundation/journal/Spring10/cannon.fm, accessed July 18, 2010.
6. Tony Horwitz, *Confederates in the Attic: Dispatches from the Unfinished Civil War* (New York: Pantheon Books, 1998), 126.
7. Jenny Thompson, *War Games: Inside the World of Twentieth Century War Re-enactors* (Washington: Smithsonian Books, 2004), 188.
8. Ibid., 136, quoting Ray Gill.
9. Carla Tilghman, "Giovanna Cenami's Veil: A Neglected Detail," in *Medieval Clothing and Textiles 2*, ed. Robin Netherton and Gale Owen-Crocker (Rochester, NY: Boydell & Brewer, 2005, 155–172), 168–171.
10. Horwitz, 10

11. Ian McCalman and Paul A. Pickering, "Historical Reenactment: From Realism to the Affective Term," in *Historical Reenactment: From Realism to the Affective Term*, ed. Ian McCalman and Paul A. Pickering (London: Palgrave Macmillan, 2010), 3.
12. Stephen Gapps, "On Being a Mobile Monument: Historical Re-enactment and Commemorations," in *Historical Reenactment: From Realism to the Affective Term,* ed. Ian McCalman and Paul A. Pickering (London: Palgrave Macmillan, 2010), 52.
13. McCalman and Pickering, 7–8.
14. Michael A. Cramer, *Medieval Fantasy as Performance: The Society for Creative Anachronism and the Current Middle Ages* (Lanham, MD: The Scarecrow Press, 2010), 25.
15. McCalman and Pickering, 12
16. Young, 187
17. McCalman and Pickering, 3
18. Cramer, 29, quoting Susan Carroll-Clark.
19. Thompson, xvi–xvii.
20. Patrick O'Donnell, *The Knights Next Door: Everyday People Living Middle Ages Dreams* (New York: iUniverse, 2004), 259, quoting Dan Shadrake of the British pre-Conquest group Britannia.
21. Thompson, 118. Thompson, who studied primarily World War II re-enactors, writes that infiltration of German re-enactment units by modern neo-Nazis was a constant concern.
22. Ibid., 115. Thompson describes the risible impression created by a group of overweight white men personifying a Japanese combat unit.
23. O'Donnell, 263–264
24. John Triggs, "The Past Belongs To Us All," in *Unlocking the Past: Celebrating Historical Archaeology in North America*, ed. Lu Ann De Cunzo & John H. Jameson, Jr. (University Press of Florida: Gainesville, 2005, 194–199), 198.
25. Cramer, 19
26. Thompson, 245
27. An excellent example of study without re-creation is Gail Marsh's *18th Century Embroidery Techniques*, published in 2006 by the Guild of Master Craftsmen in the United Kingdom. Marsh, former curator of the Rachel Kay-Shuttleworth needlework collection at Gawthorpe Hall in British, gives instructions for recreating lost embroidery techniques such as Hollie Point, diagrams of period stitches, and advice on examining a piece of historic needlework, all without the slightest indication that she is writing for anyone but modern embroidery enthusiasts.
28. Drea Leed, " 'Ye Shall Have It Cleane': Textile Cleaning Techniques in Renaissance Europe," in *Medieval Clothing and Textiles 2*, ed. Robin Netherton and Gale Owen-Crocker (Rochester, NY: Boydell & Brewer, 2006), 119.
29. Carla Tilghman, "Giovanna Cenami's Veil: A Neglected Detail," in *Medieval Clothing and Textiles 1*, ed. Robin Netherton and Gale Owen-Crocker (Rochester, NY: Boydell & Brewer, 2005), 168–171.
30. Lois Swales and Heather Blatt, "Tiny Textiles Hidden in Books: Toward a Categorization of Multiple-Strand Bookmarkers," in *Medieval Clothing and Textiles 3*, ed. Robin Netherton and Gale Owen-Crocker (Rochester, NY: Boydell & Brewer, 2007, 145–180), *passim*.
31. Janet Arnold, with additional material by Jenny Tiramani and Santina M. Levey, *Patterns of Fashion 4: The Cut and Construction of Linen Shirts, Smocks, Neckwear, Headwear and Accessories for Men and Women c. 1540–1660* (London: Pan Macmillan Ltd., 2008), 126–127. In addition to a section showing how to make, starch, and set three kinds of Elizabethan neckwear, this volume also gives a list of suppliers and an annotated bibliography clearly intended for the use of re-enactors and costume technicians.
32. Rozanne Bender, interview by the author, July 12, 2010.
33. Ibid.
34. Ibid.
35. Tilghman, 169–170
36. Bender interview

37. O'Donnell, 284
38. Ibid., 262
39. O'Donnell, 268
40. Ibid., 256–257
41. O'Donnell, 263–269 *passim.*
42. Linda Matchan, "History, High-Tech, Woven Into Jacket," in *The Boston Globe,* December 10, 2009, http://www.boston.com/news/local/massachusetts/articles/2009/12/10/plimoth_plantation_reproduces_17th_century_embroidered_jacket/, accessed April 30, 2012.
43. Tricia Wilson Nguyen, "The Embroiderers' Story Blog." http://www.thistle-threads.com/embroidery/ebsblog/index.html, accessed May 4, 2012.
44. Laura Mellin, "Extreme Costuming: Home." www.extremecostuming.com, accessed May 3, 2012. Mellin belongs to several groups, including Gardiner's Company, Trayn'd Bandes of London, and the SCA, where she goes by the name "Isobel Bedingfield."
45. Ibid., "An Elizabeth Embroidered Jacket." http://www.extremecostuming.com/reproductions/themaidstonejacket.html, retrieved May 3, 2012.
46. Jerome de Groot, *Consuming History: Historians and Heritage in Popular Culture* (London: Routledge, 2009), 105–106.
47. The book *Hidden in Plain View,* by Jacqueline Tobin and Raymond Dobard, first popularized this theory. Despite repeated and thorough debunkings by quilt historians such as Barbara Brackman, Leigh Fellner, and Patricia Cummings, the idea that escaping slaves used patchwork quilts to guide them to freedom has become an American myth comparable only to the belief that George Washington chopped down a cherry tree.

GLASS ON FIRE:
TEMPERATURES IN RECONSTRUCTED VIKING-ERA BEAD FURNACES

Neil Peterson with Sarah Backa, Jean Ross, and Robert Schweitzer

Glass beads were a widely used form of Viking era Norse personal ornamentation. Seven production sites have been found archaeologically, although only Ribe, Denmark has well-documented traces of furnaces. Using data from the excavations and experimental archaeology, three possible charcoal-fired cob furnace reconstructions were tested, with particular emphasis on temperature patterns and ranges. Over the past three years, the authors of this paper and other members of the Dark Ages Re-creation Company have been working to create a furnace that will produce glass beads reliably while being consistent with the few archaeological finds and technology level of the Viking Era Scandinavian world.

Due to the limited number of artifacts, re-creating a functional bead furnace has required extensive preliminary experimentation. Our initial experiments involved a lot of trial and error as we became comfortable with the basic techniques involved and the differences between those techniques and the modern skills.

This paper will outline the archaeological evidence and a sequence of experiments designed to explore the relationship between furnace structure and temperature. This paper represents a partial look at an ongoing sequence of experiments. There are numerous variables that have not yet been taken into account, and the sequence is far from complete at this time.

Summary of Extant Remains

The processes behind making glass and glass beads leave behind diagnostic material. At this point in time there have been no archaeological remains that point to the production of glass in any of the regions controlled by the Norse.

The production of glass beads leaves behind raw materials, semi-manufactures, broken and whole beads, and tools. This production debris has been found at a total of eight locations: Ahus, Birka, Fröjel, Hedeby, Helgo, Kaupang, Paviken and Ribe. The reproduction furnaces draw heavily on the Ribe site as it is the only well documented occurrence of remains of the furnaces (Figure 1).

The raw material for glass bead making is found as tesserae or sherds. Of the eight sites listed, six have the raw material in one of those two forms. At Ribe for example over 400 tesserae were found.[1] Analysis such as Henderson's examination of the glass at Borg suggest sources from Italy, Israel, or Greece for the raw glass indicating substantial trade networks.[2]

In its raw form, glass can be easily worked in a number of ways. Experimentally we have found that it can be directly worked into beads. Using a crucible such as those found at Paviken and Helgo the raw material can be melted.[3] By reaching into the crucible with a pair of tweezers and slowly drawing the tweezers back a rod of glass can be drawn from the liquid glass. Varying the speed of the draw will change the size of the rod produced. In the archaeological record this

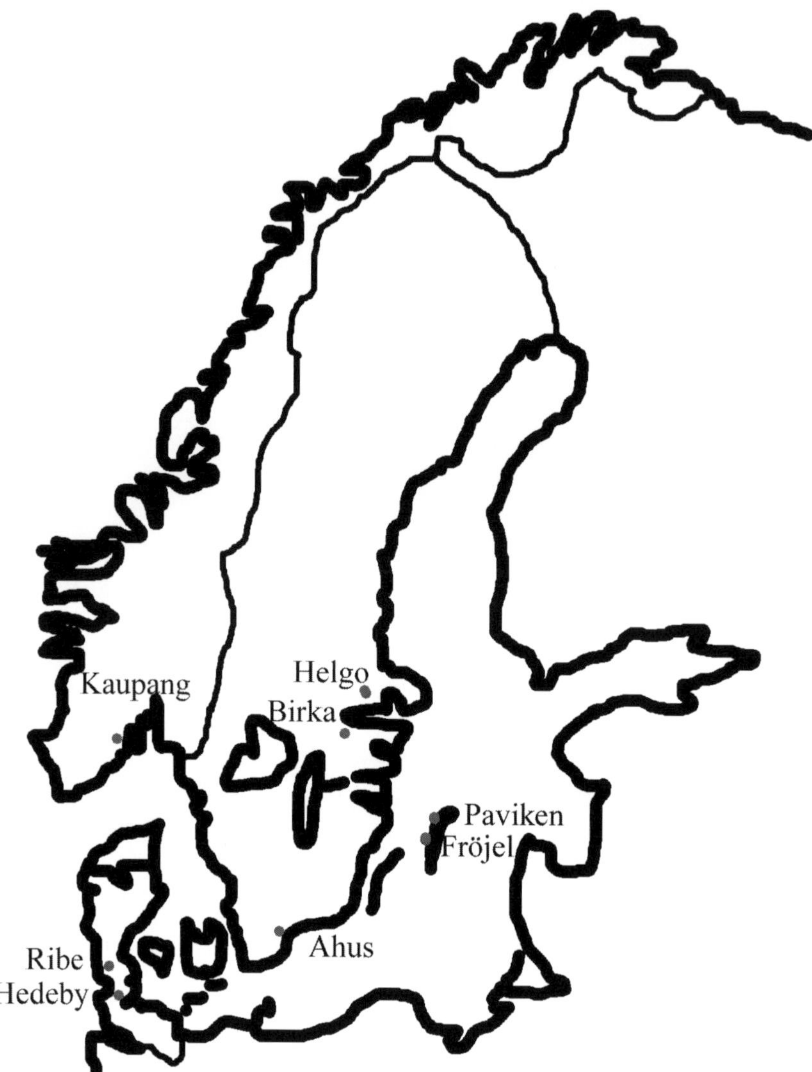

Figure 1

produces small lumps of glass with tweezer marks and small stubs of rods attached (see Figure 2). These rods can be used to directly create beads in a style strongly related to modern lampworking techniques. The rods can be put together to form different patterns (Figure 5) and then used as decoration on beads like Callmer's B017. Finally, the rods can be combined in much more complex patterns such as checkerboards, spirals, and eyes (Figure 6), broken into thin slices, and used to decorate or make beads such as Callmer's G002. Examples of all of these types of rods have been found at Ahus and Ribe.[4]

The process of making beads inevitably leads to broken beads. Annealing problems, enclosed air bubbles, and mistakes in winding the beads can lead to beads chipping or splitting. While glass wasn't cheap, it was certainly not cost effective to try and recover all the fragments. This results in a debris field surrounding the area in which the bead manufacturer worked.

A cursory examination of the types of flaws seen in the artifacts is encouraging in that we saw virtually identical break patterns in our own bead production.

Figure 2: Artifact drawn rods, tesserae, and end lumps with tweezer marks from Gotland. The rods can also be twisted together to form reticella (Figure 3), which can be used in beads (Figure 4) such as Callmer's B422 or K001. (Photo by Neil Peterson, 2011; bead production fragments Gotland Historical Museum, Sweden. Remaining photos are modern reproductions by the authors.)

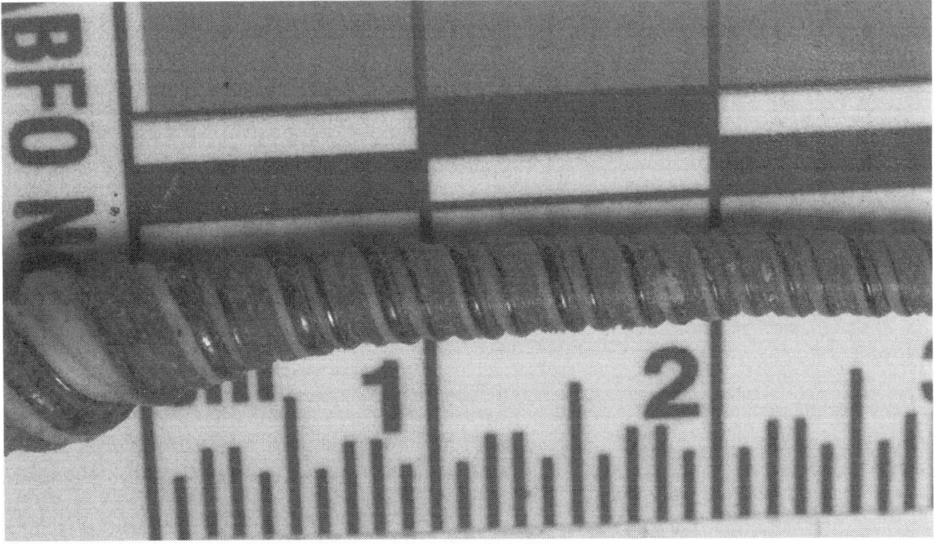

Figure 3: A reproduction reticella rod formed in a bead furnace

Figure 4: A reproduction bead made by applying reticella to a preformed bead

Figure 5: Reproduction complex patterned glass rods, with beads

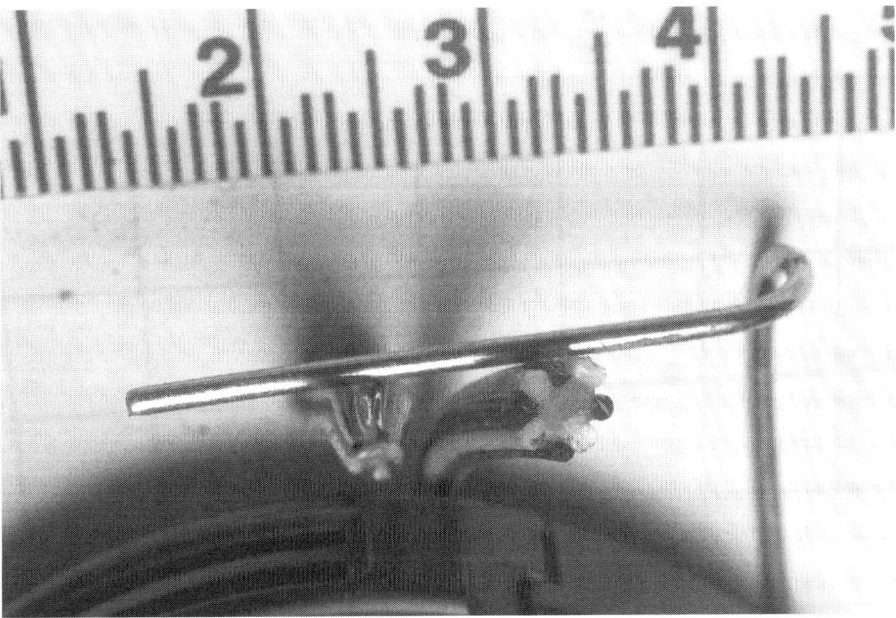

Figure 6: Reproduction millefiore rod suitable for making eyes on beads

Very little evidence has been found of the furnaces. Torben Sode indicated that Callmer may have found hearths at Ahus but at publication we had been unable to track down any citation with this information.[5] At Ribe, at least six hearths associated with bead production debris were uncovered.

Hearth ÆZ is roughly oval at 53 by 23 cm.[6] QA is a round lens shaped hearth approximately 50 cm in diameter.[7] The remaining hearths are less well defined. UN is roughly rectangular;[8] UR is irregular in outline;[9] hearth Q in layer 8;[10] the hearth in section BA layers 39–42 are not identified by shape or size.[11]

Bencard, et al., define these hearths as being of a clay construction but the long section of hearth ÆZ appears more consistent with a cob construction.[12] (Cob is a material made from compressed earth, clay, or chalk that has been reinforced with straw.) The hearths also show color variations due to high temperatures (fire scarring). It is interesting to note that the discolorations closely follow the shape of the hearth with no unusual alterations, but that the outer portion of the hearth is not discolored—as if walls had prevented the heat from impacting that area of the hearth.

There is no evidence of any walls attached to these hearths. Specifically, this means that the hearths show a clear surface out to the edges without any irregularity that might indicate a point at which a wall was attached. This is somewhat problematic, as our experimentation has shown that it is very difficult to break down a furnace without leaving at least some sign of the walls—even when the walls and base were assembled separately. If the two parts are put together even slightly wet, the weight of the superstructure will form a bond with the base, and later disassembly clearly shows a vertical structure adhering to the outer edges of the base. While it is possible that the bases and walls were created and fired separately the authors have been unable to find an advantage in doing so, and the overall structure is weaker for the walls not being joined at the bottom. Some "unburnt clay" was found above some charcoal on hearth UR and may be remains of walls or crucibles.[13]

The bases all appear to be located at ground level with no trace of a plinth or elevated pedestal, or pit features in the surrounding area. Hearth QA provides the strongest evidence for these hearths being created and fired in situ. This hearth is lens shaped thinning to the edges. Radial cracks run inwards from the circumference covering perhaps half of the distance towards the center. It is difficult to see how this hearth could have been fired on a raised platform or support and then, when it had cooled, been placed on the ground without several of the pieces at the edge breaking away from the main body. Our own experience, which appears to match that recorded by Sode at Purdalapur and in Turkey, find it preferable to be seated with the working zone at least 40 cm off the ground to create good working sightlines.[14] To accomplish this, pits for our legs were dug beside the furnace with the spoil being used to create a plinth for the furnaces. This created a workable set-up that provided easy access to both the interior of the furnace and the chimneys. The bead maker employed at the Ribe museum uses a similar setup today.[15] Unfortunately this setup cannot be supported by the archaeology. While it is possible that Viking-era bead manufacturers may have made the beads in a squatting position, similar to that still used by bead makers in Turkey and Africa today, this does not address the issue of the sightlines. Those modern furnaces still have the working ports significantly elevated, which would yield an unstable design on the small hearth size used by the Viking Era Scandinavians.

Construction of the Experimental Furnaces

The bead group has run several experimental sequences over the course of our years of work. In preparing for this temperature sequence, it was decided to use a similar medium for the construction of all the furnaces. All of the furnaces were created with clay powder (either Bell Dark or Redart) mixed 1:1 with horse manure. Horses are extremely efficient at breaking straw into the appropriate size needed and when dry, manure breaks down into almost a powder with straw.

Straight clay furnaces inevitably cracked due to the stress of the temperature variations. The short straw bits in the cob worked to maintain the structural integrity of the furnaces even when cracking occurred. The straw also helped out in drying out the furnaces. In straight clay structures, the production of steam as a furnace dries can lead to spalling as pockets of steam in the walls explode due to the pressure build-up. The straw allows the water to wick away from the inside of the walls. It is important to note that the evaporation process is endothermic. This means that until the furnace is completely dried (a process that can take hours at operational temperatures), the furnace's temperature will be reduced significantly. This was proven to be true even after a new furnace was left to dry for a week prior to firing. For this reason the furnaces used for graphical analysis during a heating cycle were fired and sample temperatures taken a number of days in advance.

Five furnaces were created in the most recent series of experiments, each with one big or two small changes in order to examine different ideas. Of these furnaces (generally named for their primary architect), three were digitally monitored for at least one heating cycle. The first furnace, "Wendi" filled most of a 30cm by 60cm kiln plate and was over 30 cm tall. Each end had a large chimney centered in that half with a port cut into each end. Air was added through a tuyere in the center of one long side. A large diverter (wedge of cob on the inner wall facing the tuyere) split the incoming air creating two working fire zones—one on each end. Just above this wedge, a large chute for loading charcoal was built into the furnace. A lid covered the chute when the furnace was in use. An annealing pot was built between the two chimneys. This represented our "baseline" furnace from previous experiments.

Figure 7: The "Wendi" furnace

A lot of heat was lost through the charcoal chute and it made for hot work when using the furnace. This had also been noted with previous furnaces and the use of such chutes was discontinued after this furnace.

"Karen" was built narrow for the length (25 cm) with very thick walls (5 cm). Two ports were at opposite ends with the floor of the ports being cut in a tooth manner for holding the mandrels. This was for ease of use and was appreciated differently by each bead-maker. There were two small chimneys with a long and narrow crucible between them. The crucible was not very deep. This furnace produced less sparks in general when lit. It is not currently known if the shape or wall thickness contributed to this, further experimentation is required.

Figure 8: The "Karen" furnace

These two furnaces were excluded from the remainder of the recording sequence, but they did generate temperatures over 800 °C in the chimneys and 1000 °C in the ports.

The "Sarah" was smaller than the "Wendi," but of our usual shape and style. It had two ports, only one chimney and no chute. Charcoal was put into the furnace through the chimney or ports. A standard diverter was placed post-completion of the furnace and seemed to do the job quite well. "Sarah" had a large, deep crucible mounted on the outside of the long wall opposite the tuyere. The changes noted are the smaller size, single chimney, deeper crucible, and removal of the charging chute.

Figure 9: The "Sarah" furnace

"Goderich" was between the sizes of "Wendi" and "Sarah." It still had two chimneys but with a pronounced diverter, and no charging chute. The ports were at the ends of the furnace, but were cut on different angles. The port that was cut on an angle up into the furnace seemed to produce less escaped heat. The other port was cut at an angle down into the furnace which allowed escaping heat to affect the beadmaker. This proved to be only important for the beadmaker and did not influence temperature or production.

"Neil" was very different from the other body styles, being based on hearth QA instead of ÆZ as the others were. It was a round shape fitting neatly onto a 30cm slate tile. It is affectionately known as a "teapot" style as it somewhat resembled one. It had thick walls and the tuyere was high on the side. The port was also very high up the opposite side leaving quite a large bowl inside. No diverter was needed, although the tuyere was directed at an angle towards the side wall of the oven. A chimney topped the furnace. The crucible was deep and wall mounted between tuyere and port.

Figure 10: The "Goderich" furnace

Figure 11: The "Neil" Furnace

Experimental Background

Once we were able to successfully produce beads on a reliable basis, we started to refine the furnace designs that worked. Very early on, it became apparent that the charcoal was an important part of the equation. The temperatures in the "working areas" of the furnace (chimneys and just inside the ports) would only remain above the melting point of the glass for a short period of time before the charcoal would be burnt and the temperatures started to drop dramatically. Softwood charcoal burned quite hot, but wouldn't last long enough to provide time to produce many beads. If the charcoal was "dusty" (contained fine particulates), there would be a lot of sparks produced, which could be damaging to both bead and artisan. For this reason these experiments were conducted with a single brand of hardwood lump charcoal.

The glass used for these experimental beads was Moretti 104. This is a "soft" glass that has a melting point of approximately 700° Celsius or 1300° Fahrenheit. Experimentally we noticed that the glass could be worked below 700° C although it was easier to work above that temperature, especially in the early part of the bead creation. The use of a single type of glass reduced the experimental complexity by limiting the glass to a single coefficient of expansion.[16] The melting point and coefficient of expansion are affected by impurities in the silica (sand) used to make the glass. Since the Scandinavians were obtaining their glass from multiple sources, it is uncertain what range of values with which they were working, and whether the different COE's would require special techniques. Further analysis of the COE and melting points of Viking Era glass may lead to additional experimental sequences in the future.

As it is likely that external environmental conditions played a part in the recorded data it is worth recording the following information. On September 11th the local weather was 60% humidity, 24.5° C, pressure of 101.5 KPa with around half meter per second winds. On the 17th of September the weather was 45% humidity, 16° C pressure of 100.7 KPa with calm winds. Finally on the 10th of October the weather was 60–100% humidity, as low as 8° C, with a pressure of 102.4 KPa, winds variable from 0 to 2 m/s and a drizzly rain.

Analysis of Results

Temperatures were recorded for the furnaces on the 11th and 17th of September and 10th of October 2011. This was done by placing a J/K Thermocouple in various locations. The September burn temperatures were taken from the chimneys only, while the October burn temperatures were recorded from two locations the port and the chimney. It must be noted that the port temperatures were taken with the port being closed, and therefore would not necessarily be the temperatures seen if the ports were open and used as a working area for bead manufacture. Also, since the ports were not opened for use, and the tests were run with an electrical air source as opposed to the hand-powered bellows, the temperature could not be altered by the internal manipulation of charcoal or noticeable changes in airflow. All temperatures are recorded in Celsius, and the graphs were produced by taking a temperature every 5 seconds. Gaps in the data occurred in a few intervals when the person using the furnace obscured the view of the temperature readout.

Other factors involved when discussing burn times, are the differences between temperature-defined workable windows, and user-defined workable windows. This can vary for a variety of reasons, such as how "sparky" the furnace is being, wind strength and direction, and the comfort level of the user in regards to these factors. The working window for the furnaces was determined by the length of time between the temperature surpassing 700° C, and dropping below 600° C in the chimneys. The chimneys were used for the benchmark, as that was the location used for the majority of the bead work done using the furnaces themselves. As such, the ports were not used during the recordings and it can be assumed that the recorded temperatures would have been different if the ports were open and in use. The time to heat was calculated from the end of the addition of charcoal until the chimney temperature passed 700° C.

In all of the furnaces, the expected "load, crash, raise" temperature pattern was witnessed. The charcoal was loaded into a heated furnace, the temperature crashed, and then rose fairly steadily as the charcoal began to ignite.

The "Neil" furnace shows significant variation between the September and October burn. In the September burn, the furnace took 1:20 minutes to come to a working temperature, and remained in the working zone for 10:45 minutes. It reached a maximum of 1070° C in the chimney, and 962° C at the port. It can be noted that this burn shows two different loadings of charcoal. This was done because it was discovered after the burn began that working temperatures were not being reached. It was discovered that the charcoal had formed a bridge within the furnace, leading to a large air pocket. This meant that there was significantly less charcoal than necessary, and more was added. After this was done, the necessary temperature was achieved.

During the October burn, it took one minute to reach the required temperature at the chimney. The temperatures within the chimney generally remained within the working range for 3 minutes 55 seconds, peaking at 669° C. The temperatures at the port reached 600° C after 3m 10s, reached a peak temperature of 923° C after 7m 20s, and remained above 800° C until the air was cut off at the 10m 5s mark.

It is important to note that while the October burn did not reach the same temperature levels as in September, the temperatures were more consistent and did not drop off as severely. This may be due to the change in the angle of the truyure between the two dates. In the October burn, the tuyere was positioned at an angle of 15 degrees from the normal, which aimed the airflow around the edges of the oven.

The "Sarah" furnace also shows some variation in temperature between our two recorded tests, but shows a generally more consistent result. The furnace took forty-five seconds to one minute to reach our working zone temperature, although the furnace had a tendency to run somewhat "sparky" initially, and therefore the available working time and the length of recorded working temperature show a difference of approximately a minute. During the September burn, it remained at a working temperature for 11m 35s, while in October, it stayed at a working temperature for a much shorter time of 6m 10s. The maximum recorded temperature for the chimney was 837° C at the 2m 30s mark, and the maximum temperature taken at the port was 1160° C at 5m 5s. A temperature of over 800° C after being established, was maintained at the ports until the working temperature had been lost in the chimney and the burn was ceased.

The "Goderich" furnace, as expected, both took longer to reach a working temperature, and maintained that temperature for longer than any of the smaller furnaces. During the September burn, Goderich took 3m 50s to reach a working temperature, and remained there for 18m 50s. During the October burn, it took 1m 40s to reach a working temperature in the chimney. Chimney temperature peaked at 914° C after 4m 25s. It should be noted that the Goderich furnace reached working temperature at the ports within 5 seconds of the burn beginning, and remained above the working temperature until the bellows were shut off. It reached a maximum temperature of 1031° C after 4m 35s. The temperature remained within the working zone for 8m 25s. The meter also shut off during this recording, leading to loss of some information. It should be noted that Goderich was run using hand-powered bellows during the September 17th burn,[17] rather than the electrical air sources used

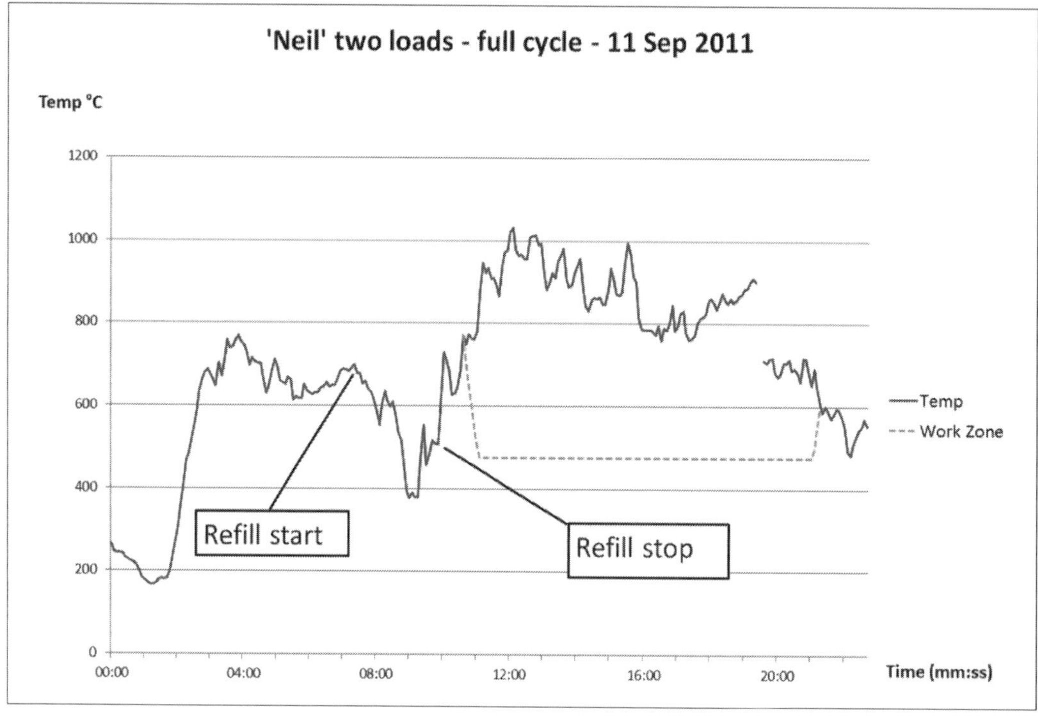

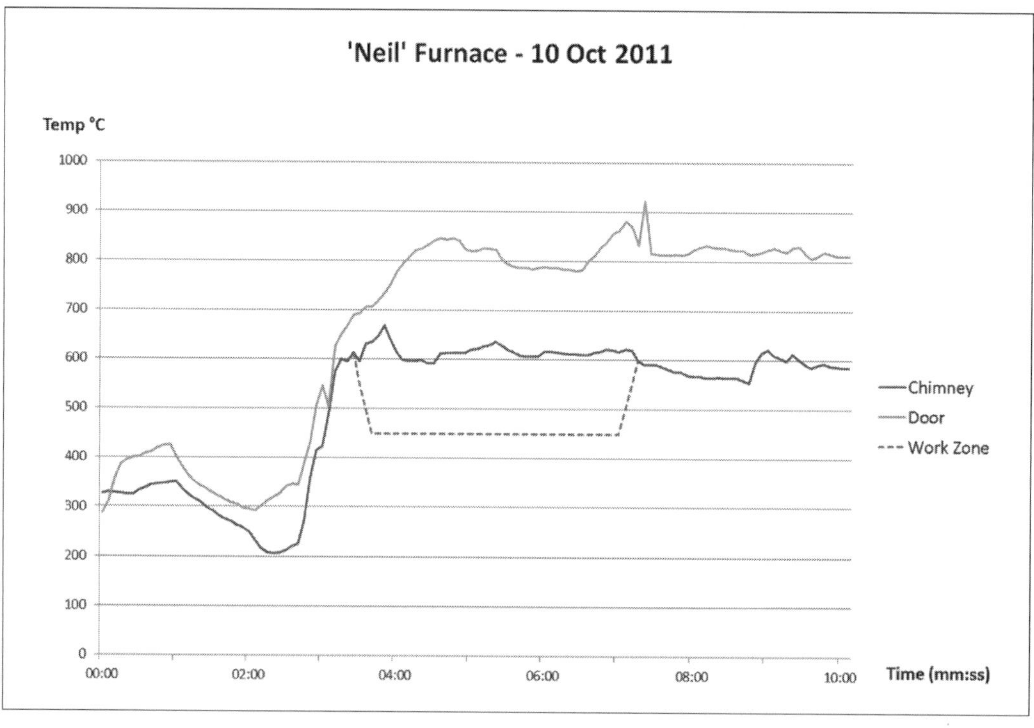

Figures 12 and 13: Temperature graphs for the "Neil" furnace

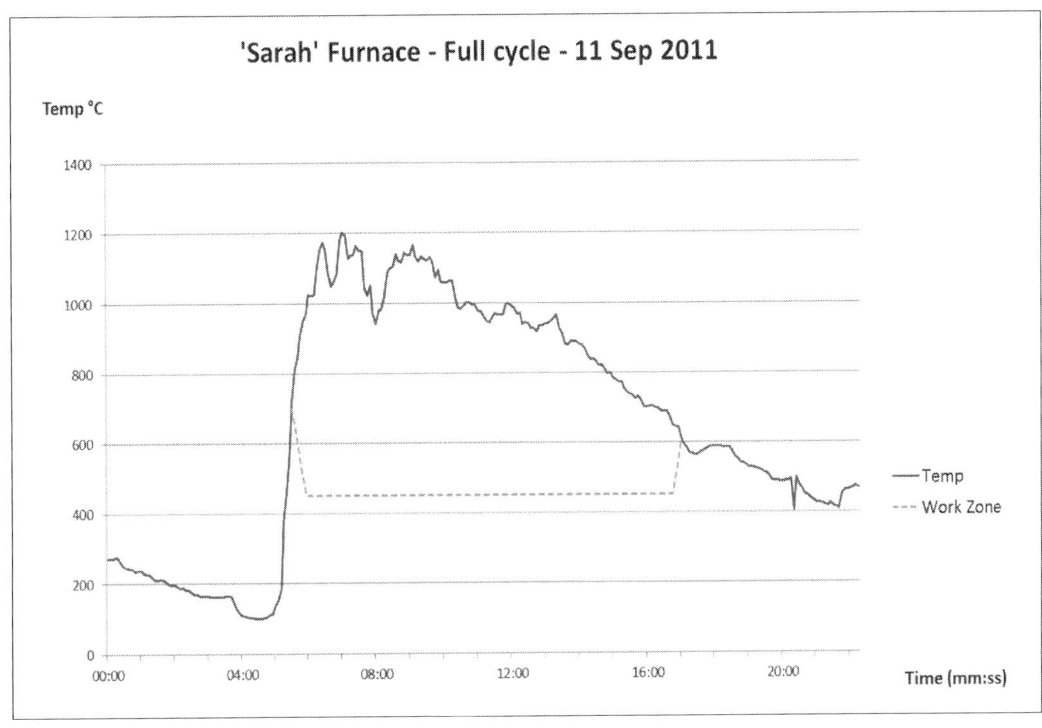

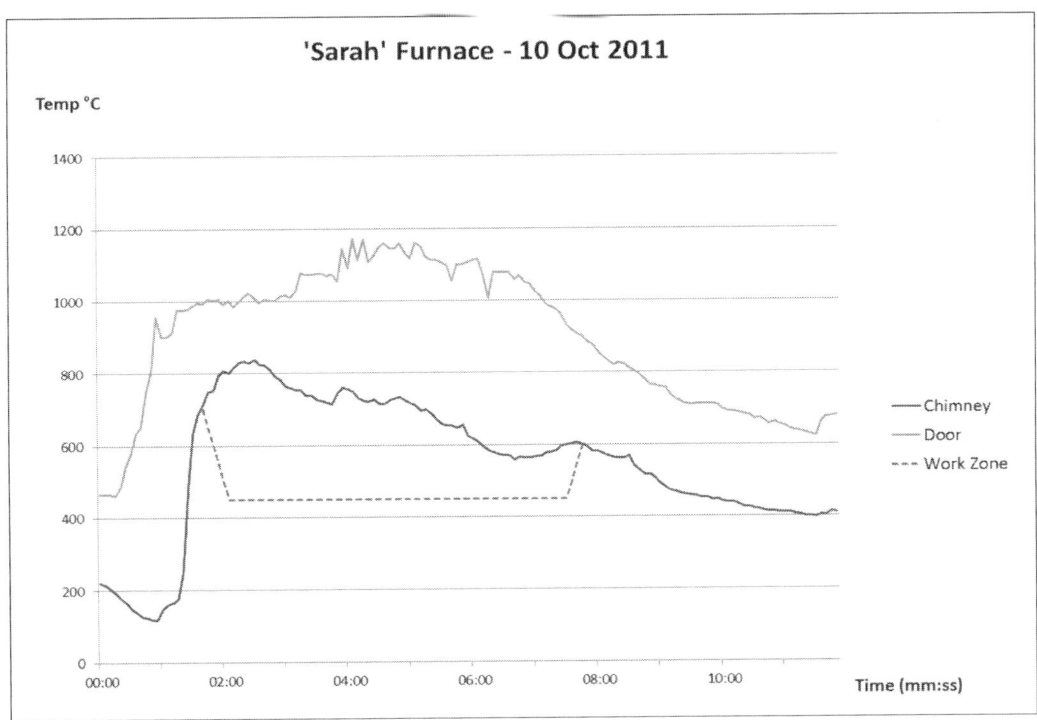

Figures 14 and 15: Temperature graphs for the "Sarah" furnace

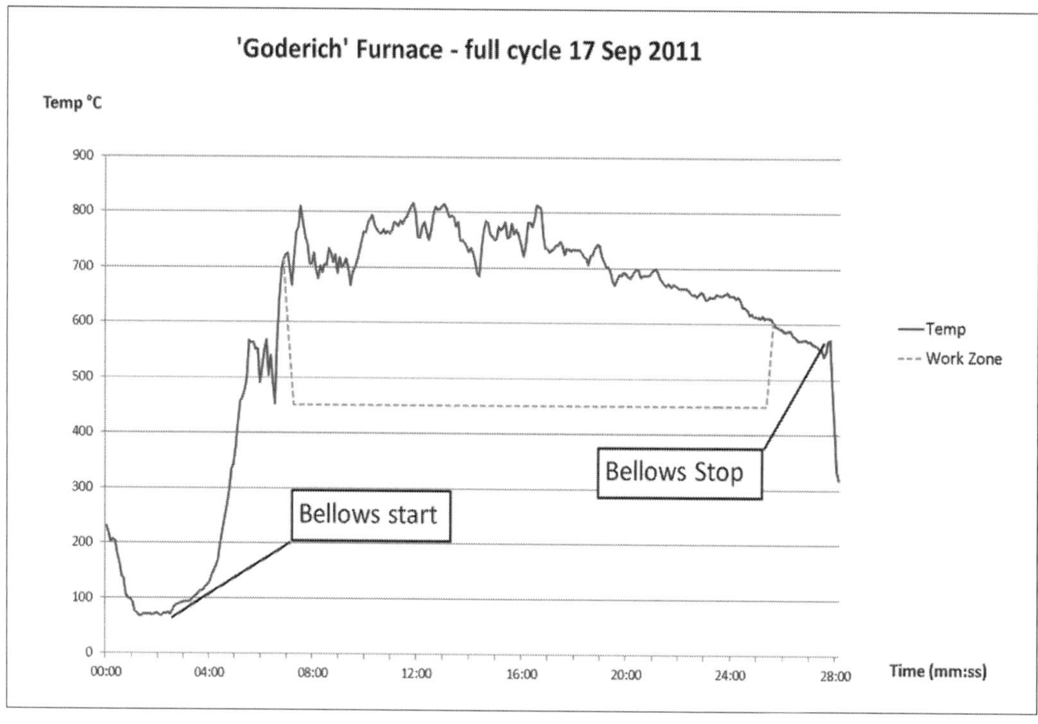

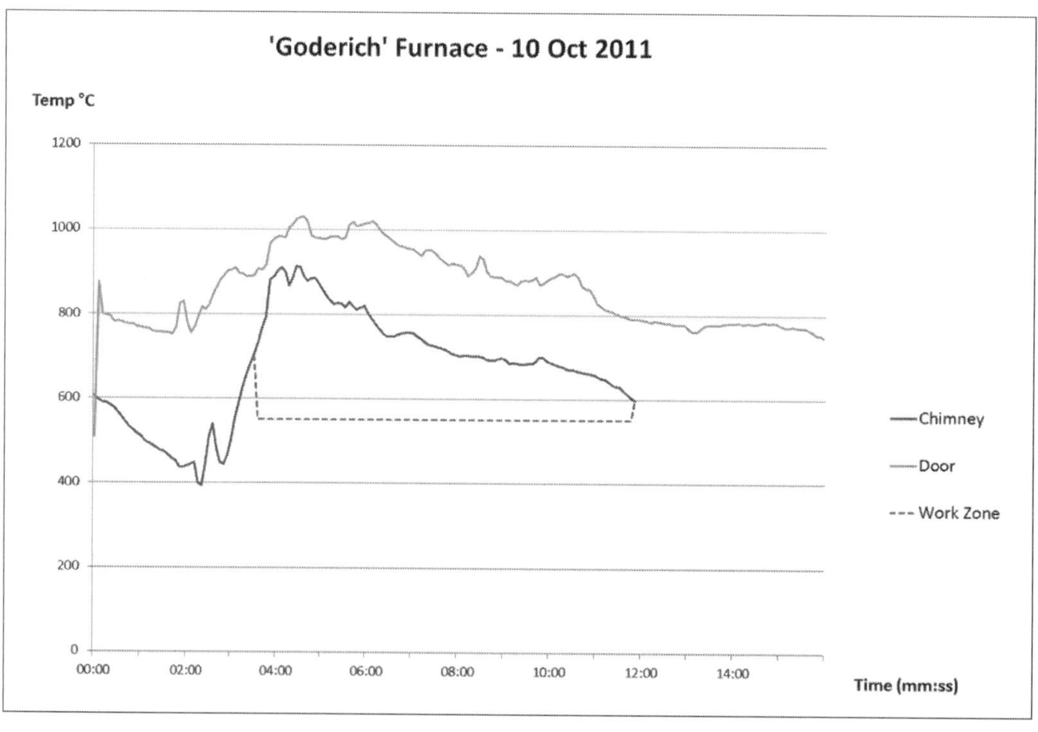

Figures 16 and 17: Temperature graphs for the "Goderich" furnace

during the other weekends. This led to lower than expected temperatures in the chimney (peaking at 816° C after 11m 50s), and a longer than expected window of workable temperatures with far less fluctuation in temperature. This might have been due to the communication between the person using the furnace and the person working the bellows to better control airflow, being able to increase or decrease airflow to maintain the minimal necessary temperature, and avoid stirring up ash.

Conclusions

Any of the bead furnace shapes and sizes produced for this sequence are capable of producing the environment required to create beads similar to those created by the Viking Era Scandinavians.

The graphs clearly demonstrate a fairly consistent 200-degree difference between the oven and the chimney. For the beadmaker this can be useful, as it allows the use of the chimney for fine work using thin rods that melt readily, while the inner oven is used for melting large amounts of glass more efficiently. The graphs also show a significant drop in temperature as the charcoal is consumed. The primary cause of the differences in the rate of temperature decreases is uncertain, although environmental conditions and oven structure are the main considerations.

This experimental sequence was clearly impacted by external environmental factors. For this reason it would be worth repeating the sequence using additional people and running all furnaces multiple times in a single day. If these runs are combined with recording the weight of charcoal used in each run, a preliminary estimate of the efficiency of each design could be determined.

We are still experiencing significantly more ash damage on our beads than are seen on the original beads. When combined with the sparks discussed earlier this indicates that more attention needs to be focused on the charcoal itself. The iron smelting experiments conducted by DARC use a more precisely sized charcoal.[18] Repeating the experiments with sized charcoal could provide useful information to complement the efficiency numbers described above.

As with the size of charcoal, iron smelters change their behavior significantly depending on the airflow. Adding inline airflow and pressure meters would add another layer to the efficiency dataset. There also needs to be a more detailed analysis of the effect of structure on airflow. Since the change in the angle of the tuyere in the "Neil" furnace seemed to have a strong regulating affect, this needs further investigation. This tends to imply that developing a similar circular airflow pattern in the two-person oval ovens would create a more efficient burn.

In deconstructing the furnaces after these experiments, several observations are worth recording. In all cases the locations of the walls was clear on the bases. This is a significant visual and construction difference from the hearths found at Ribe.

In addition, the fire scarring on the furnaces did not match the hearths at Ribe. Hearth QA has a clear circular fire scar pattern. The "Neil" had an off-center scarring that went part way up the right wall while leaving part of the base untouched. It is possible that the scar on this furnace was offset as the air was pushed in on an angle to reduce the air volume. It is also possible that the position of the scar was altered by the use of the door on the right wall.

While hearth ÆZ is only slightly discolored it does seem to show as a more oval shape. The "Sarah" and "Goderich" furnaces had a pattern that showed as more of a "U" shape around the air splitter. This seems to imply that ÆZ did not include a diverter, and that it may have had the tuyere placed off to one side.

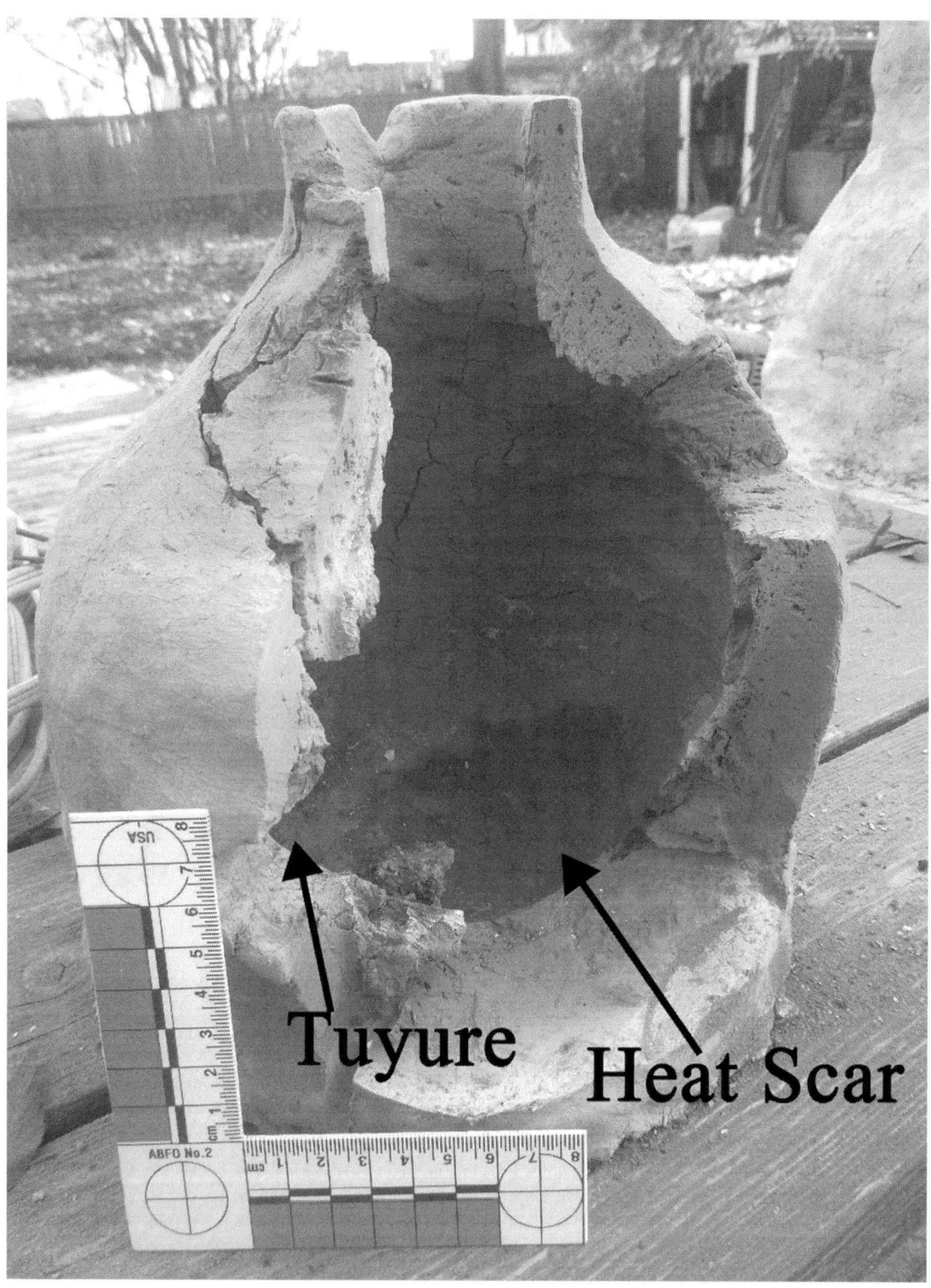

Figure 18: The heat scarring in the "Neil" furnace

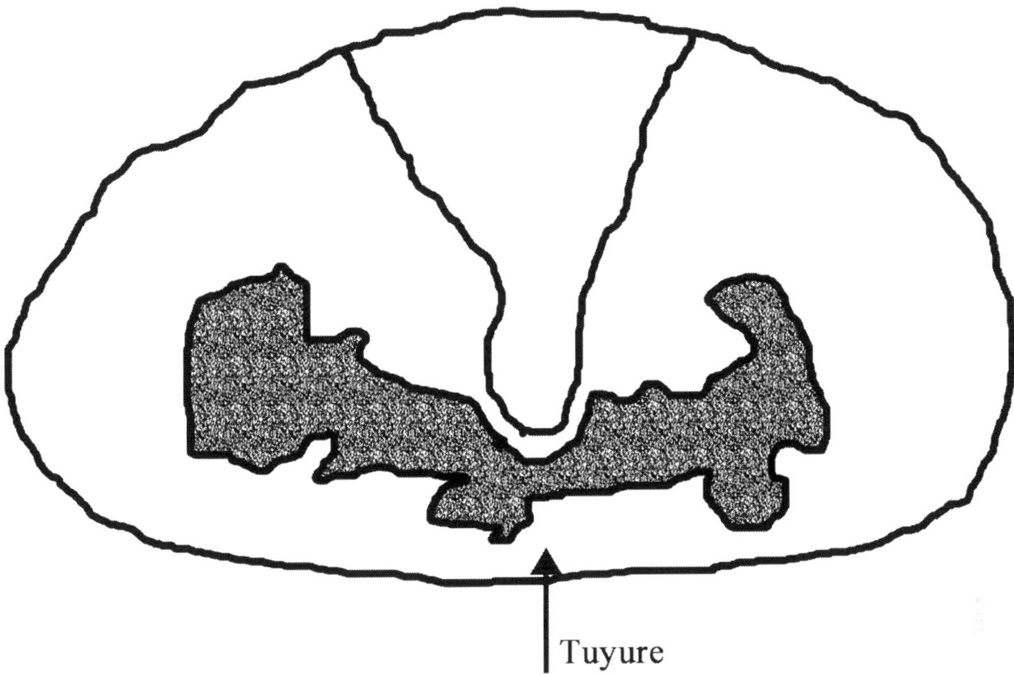

Figure 19: The heat scarring on the "Sarah" furnace

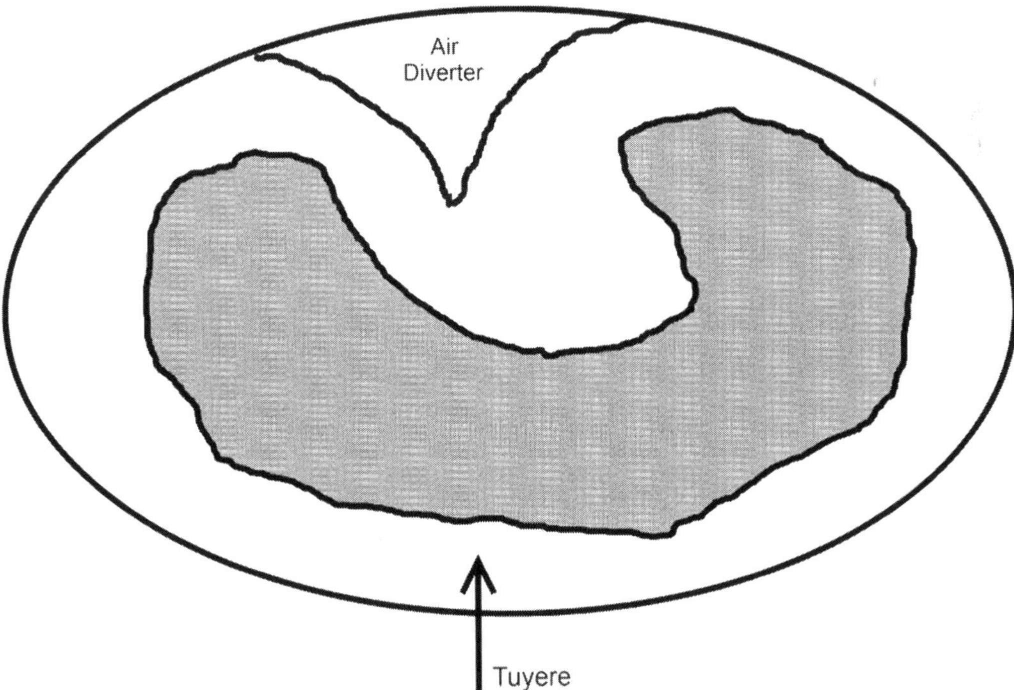

Figure 20: The heat scarring on the 'Goderich' furnace

Although the furnaces used in these experiments will clearly produce beads, they fail the primary test of experimental archaeology—they do not match the archaeological evidence. For that reason the next experimental sequence will focus on finding solutions that more closely match that evidence. Questions of efficiency and clean bead production will wait until the overall shape and construction is better understood. Additional experiments are required to facilitate a deeper investigation into the skills and techniques needed to produce the complex beads of the Norse.

Endnotes

1. Mogens Bencard and Helge Brinch Madsen, *Ribe Excavations 1970–1976,* vol. 6 (Højbjerg: Jutland Archaeology Society, 2010), 33.
2. Julian Henderson and Ingegerd Holand, "The Glass from Borg, an Early Medieval Chieftain's Farm in Northern Norway," *Medieval Archaeology* 36 (1992): 92.
3. Agneta Lundström, "Bead Making in Scandinavia in the Early Middle Ages", Early Medieval Studies 9, *Antivariskt Arkiv* 61 (1976).
4. Johan Callmer and Julian Henderson, "Glassworking at Ahus, South Sweden [Skane, 8th century AD]," *Labortaiv Arkeologi* 5 (1991): 143–154; Jensen Stig, *The Vikings of Ribe* (Ribe: Den antivariske Samling, 1991), 38.
5. Personal communication with the authors, April, 2012.
6. Mogens Bencard and Helge Brinch Madsen, *Ribe Excavations 1970–1976,* vol. 4 (Højbjerg: Jutland Archaeology Society, 1990), 95 and figs. 54–56; Mogens Bencard and Helge Brinch Madsen, *Ribe Excavations 1970–1976,* vol. 5 (Højbjerg: Jutland Archaeology Society, 2004), 84.
7. Bencard and Madsen vol. 4, 99–102 and fig. 60; vol. 5, 86
8. Bencard and Madsen vol. 4, 99 and figs. 58–59; vol. 5, 84
9. Bencard and Madsen vol. 4, 99 and fig. 57; vol. 5, 84
10. Bencard and Madsen vol. 5, 84
11. Bencard and Madsen vol. 4, pl. I table 2; vol. 5, 84
12. Bencard and Madsen vol. 4, fig. 55
13. Bencard and Madsen vol. 5, 84
14. Torbin Sode and Jan Kock, *Glass, Glassbeads and Glassmakers in Northern India* (Vanlose: Thot Press, 1994).
15. Trine Theut, personal communication with the authors, 2006.
16. Glass made with different trace elements may expand and contract different amounts when heating and cooling. Mixing glasses with differing COEs when making a bead can cause the finished product to break when cooling.
17. The authors of the paper wish to thank members of the Society for Creative Anachronism who have helped out with some of the construction, and with willing assistance during bellows powered test runs.
18. See http://www.darkcompany.ca/iron, accessed April 5, 2014.

AN IRON SMELT IN VINLAND: AN EXPERIMENTAL INVESTIGATION

Darrell Markewitz

Investigations of the archaeological site at L'Anse aux Meadows, Newfoundland, indicate local bog iron ore was smelted into workable metal, at least once, by the Norse some time about 1000 AD. Starting in 2009, a team from Ontario, Canada, conducted a series of five experiments, culminating on a full re-creation of the original Norse iron smelt at L'Anse aux Meadows NHSC in August of 2010. This paper will detail how the archaeological evidence was combined with years of experience with Norse styled furnaces to produce a successful working system. What was learned about the physical process can now shed greater light on not only early iron smelting methods, but what happened in Vinland near the end of the Viking Age.[1] It is outside the scope of this paper to rationalize the best methods to undertake a successful bloomery iron smelt. The processes undertaken are the result of a decade of practical experiments, thirty nine at the start of the Vinland series.[2]

Background: Iron at Vinland

The first iron smelted from ore in North America was produced in northern Newfoundland by the Norse some time about the year 1000.[3] Archaeological evidence of this event was uncovered by Helge and Anne Stine Ingstad in the 1960s near by the small village of L'Anse aux Meadows (LAM), at the very top of Newfoundland's Northern Peninsula.[4] To the Norse, this was a strategic location, with the Strait of Belle Isle controlling access to the entire region (what Leif Eirikson named "Vinland"). It is important to remember that the Norse occupation of "Straumsforðr" (Leif's Houses) in Vinland was never intended as an actual colonization attempt.[5] Instead, it is best to think of this collection of houses and their associated out buildings as a combination exploration base and lumber camp. Considered as an exploration base, assessment of possible resources, both locally and within the greater region, would have been of great interest to the Norse. The Norse occupation site lies at the bottom of the deep curve of Epaves Bay. An ancient shore line forms a terrace running roughly south to north, extending back about 60 meters from the water's edge then dropping into a low lying peat bog. Black Duck Brook bends around the occupation area, and cuts a channel across the terrace. Three main house complexes were built by the Norse, starting at the brook and extending for about 100 meters towards the north. On the slightly elevated southern bank of the brook were found the remains of a small dugout style building, about 3 by 3 meters in area and open on one side. Investigations of this structure indicated the presence of a bloomery iron smelting, including a possible furnace placed centrally.[6] The evidence included pieces of roasted primary bog iron ore, fragments of clay furnace wall, a hearth bottom, and a considerable quantity of iron smelting slag. Based on these remains, it is most likely only a single smelt event was undertaken. The initial estimates of possible yields of this smelt by the archaeologists are extremely rough, but the bloom mass created has been suggested at about 3 kg.[7] One important consideration is that the process of turning raw ore from bloom to working bar then to object is a multiple phase process. Individual aspects will require much different heat sources and equipment layouts. At LAM, it is clear that these phases were constructed one on top of the other, only leaving the clearest traces of the last steps in the overall sequence.

Overall Experimental Objectives

Our experimental objectives were three:

1. Can a functional bloomery furnace be constructed and operated based on the evidence from LAM?
2. What is the most likely arrangement of working equipment within the confines dictated by the LAM "Furnace Hut"?
3. Can a group of modern experimenters produce an iron bloom while working with Viking Age style equipments and methods?

A total of five individual full iron smelt experiments were undertaken, starting in May 2009 and running to August of 2010. As the series progressed, pieces of modern equipment were replaced with replicas of Viking Age types. The final smelt was mounted at L'Anse aux Meadows National Historic Site of Canada, inside the re-constructed Furnace Hut. Before the main series, three additional smelts were made while developing a suitable "bog ore analog." As many features as possible of both the smelting furnace and the working area would be based on those indicated from the archaeology at LAM. The working team had already amassed considerable practical experience in effective bloomery iron smelting method. Details lacking in the archaeology would be supplied from this working knowledge.

Furnace Construction

The archaeological remains at LAM suggested the following:

- Interior diameter (ID) of about 20 cm wall thickness of at least 10 cm in some spots
- Probably some method available for slag tapping
- Walls composed of a mixture of local clay with sand (no organics)
- Likely stones were used as exterior support.

Past experience suggested the following additional details:

- Total furnace height of roughly 55 cm plus walls likely to taper thinner towards top
- Tuyere placed 15 cm above base level
- Tuyere set at 20–25 degrees down from horizontal.

In this series, a new furnace was constructed for each smelting experiment. This allowed the final debris field created in each attempt to be compared back to that recorded at LAM. There were also some variation in construction details, and differing tuyere types, used through the series. (See the individual experiment descriptions.)

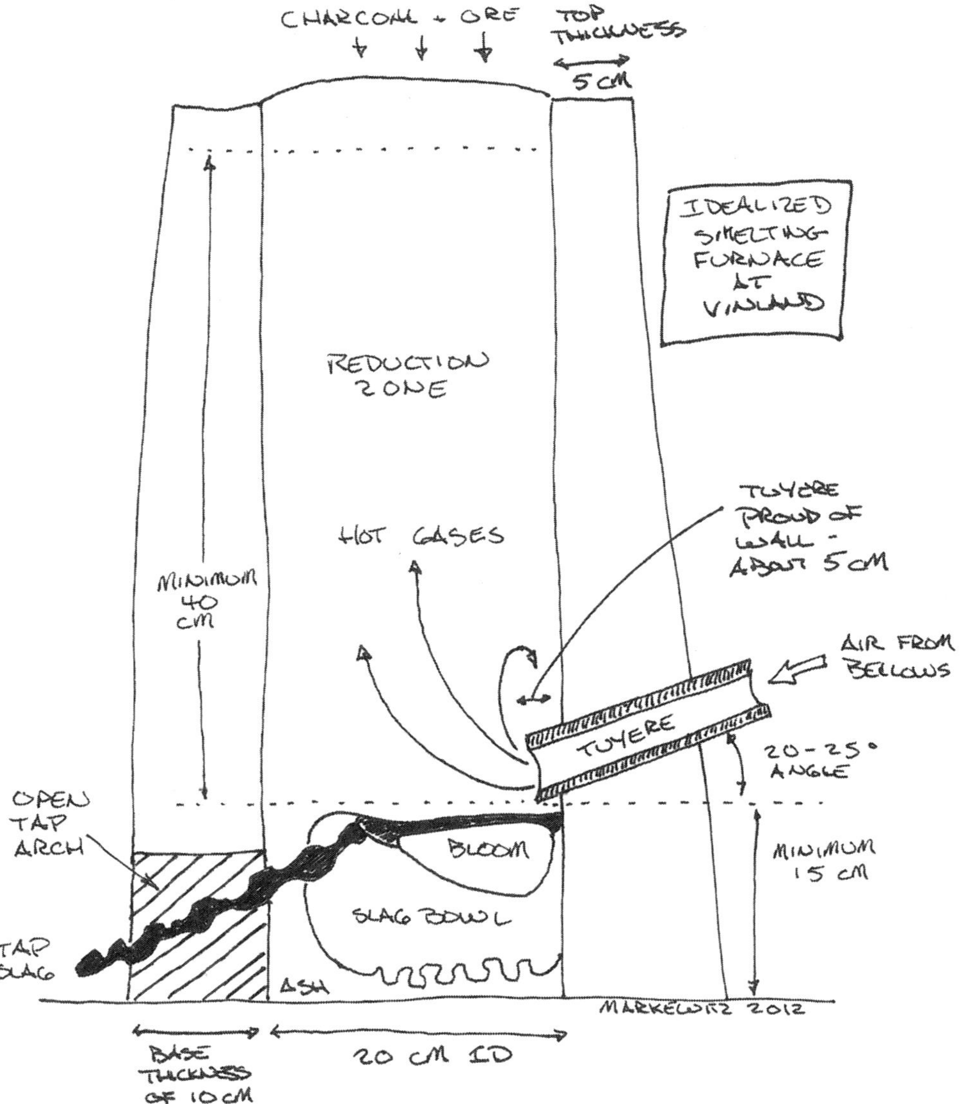

Figure 1: Idealized Vinland iron smelting furnace.

The preferred furnace wall material, over many previous furnaces, has been a mixture of powdered potter's clay with chopped straw. This cobb mixture has repeatedly proven durable and effective. However, in keeping with the wall fragments found at LAM, in this series a mixture of roughly 50/50 (by volume) powdered clay and course beach sand was used. The clay chosen was a basic stoneware type ("Bell Dark" typically) with no attempt to select for an especially high firing temperature clay body. About 45 kg of the dry clay was used for each furnace.

The starting material would be roughly mixed by hand while dry, then water added until a consistency considered suitable for wall construction was reached. This would be pinched out into lumps roughly the size of a soft ball (about 15 cm in diameter). To maintain a standard furnace size, a metal internal form (at 22 cm diameter) was used during construction.

The walls would be built up by adding courses of the individual lumps, flattened by hand first to roughly the desired wall thickness, determined by eye. As each separate batch of clay was used to build up the furnace, the metal form would be removed, and the interior space filled with a mixture of sand and ash collected from earlier smelt events. This method proved to help stabilize the lower parts of the wall as it was built taller. As well the mixture helped draw moisture out of the clay material to speed drying. In keeping with past experience, the furnaces were all constructed to a minimum height of 55 cm, higher if it proved possible.

The furnaces in this series were most typically built the day before an individual smelt attempt. Normally a small split wood fire would then be lit inside the clay cylinder to evaporate as much of the water contained in the wall material as possible. Care was required not to build up too much heat, too quickly, as the differing drying rates between inner and outer surfaces would lead to excessive cracking.

Furnaces built of this kind of sand/clay mixture require considerably more care in their construction, especially in initial drying. The end result however is a wall material with better refectory qualities (heat resistance) than the normally used straw cobb furnaces.[8] This was balanced by the fact that any given furnace would only be required to stand up to a single use. Cracking of the walls did prove to be common. These cracks would be roughly patched, an ongoing process during an individual smelt. Before the drying fire was started, the tuyere was cut and fit. The remains at LAM itself give no indication what type of tuyere might have been employed, or how it might have been positioned. Past experience has proven the ideal situation is to place the inner tip of the tuyere at roughly 15 cm above the hard base of the furnace. The tuyere is angled downwards from horizontal, with the ideal being between 20 to 25 degrees. At the start of the smelt, the tuyere tip will extend roughly 5 cm proud of the inner furnace wall. Given the specific tuyere material, and the dynamics of a given smelt, there might be considerable erosion of the tuyere and/or furnace inner wall during the firing sequence.

Over the series, both ceramic tube and steel pipe tuyeres would be used. Both types have proved successful in past smelts. The ceramic tube used was a standard 30 cm long pottery kiln shelf support. These tubes were 2 cm interior diameter with a wall thickness of 1 cm. They are sold for use in porcelain kilns, rated to a temperature of 1150 degrees Celsius. As there was no evidence from LAM of a normally durable ceramic tuyere, steel pipe (replacing wrought iron) was used for the final smelts. These were cut to 30 cm from standard 1-inch schedule 40 pipe. This provides a 2.6 cm ID with .03 cm wall thickness. Considerably more erosion was expected with the pipe tuyeres, and this would prove the case.

Air would be transferred into the tuyere from the various source equipment via a T- or Y-shaped fitting. This arrangement allows for access down the interior of the tuyere without disconnecting the air source. The primary reason this is important is to allow use of a thin rod to probe down the tuyere to clear blockages of slag.

Each furnace was also equipped with a small slag tapping arch. The most typical size was roughly 15 cm tall by 20 cm wide, set 90 degrees to the tuyere. The extraction of the bloom was planned to be made from the top of each furnace, so it was not necessary to make the arch large enough to fit the bloom and slag mass through. The arch was cut from the solid wall using a dry wall saw when the clay was still damp. The block created was then wrapped in a layer of paper and then set back in place. This prevented the furnace from slumping, but the paper kept the clay from re-fusing.

The last step of preparing any furnace was to place a number of randomly sized stone slabs against the outer wall as supports. This was undertaken primarily because the archaeologists had suggested the original Vinland furnace was constructed this way.[9] With a wall thickness of some 7–10 cm at the base and a height of roughly 55–60 cm, these furnaces were certainly stable enough on their own. First the area around the tap arch would be framed in with long rectangular stone forming a lintel. Then larger slabs would be placed to create a roughly circular box around the furnace. The space between the furnace and the stones would be filled with a loose mix of sand and ash, packing material remaining from previous smelts. One of advantage of this mixture is that it will run down into cracks that may develop in the furnace wall. On exposure to the high internal temperatures, the packing will fuse to a friable glass, helping to seal the cracks.

Working Space

The structure "Hut site J," also known as the "Furnace Hut" at LAM was dug into the southern bank of Black Duck Brook, roughly 3 meters back from the current water level of the stream. It had a width of 290 cm and depth of 320 cm, likely low side walls to support a roof, leaving the side towards the brook open.[10]

Key archaeological features within the space were:

- Overall size and open side configuration
- Central position of the furnace
- Debris suggests tapping/extraction towards the open side—presence of a shallow pit and a large stone to front left of the open side

Working equipment requirements:

- Size and placement of bellows
- Placement of a compaction surface placement of a slack tub working dynamic within the space

Coincidentally, the normal working space used for smelting experiments at Wareham proved to be almost the same size as the Furnace Hut at LAM. Temporary walls were added to the open pole roof framing to box in the space to the LAM dimensions. The furnaces were always placed as indicated at LAM, just slightly off centre. The floor area would be raked clean and a fresh layer of sand deposited before each experiment. A number of possible equipment layouts would be tested with successive smelts (described individually).

The ideal working team around the smelter had been established as three individuals:

- Smelt Master: primarily manages the conduct of the smelt, correcting problems as they occur
- Lead Hand: primarily assists the Smelt Master as required, otherwise adds ore charges
- Charcoal Worker: ensures charcoal (and ore) charges are added as required

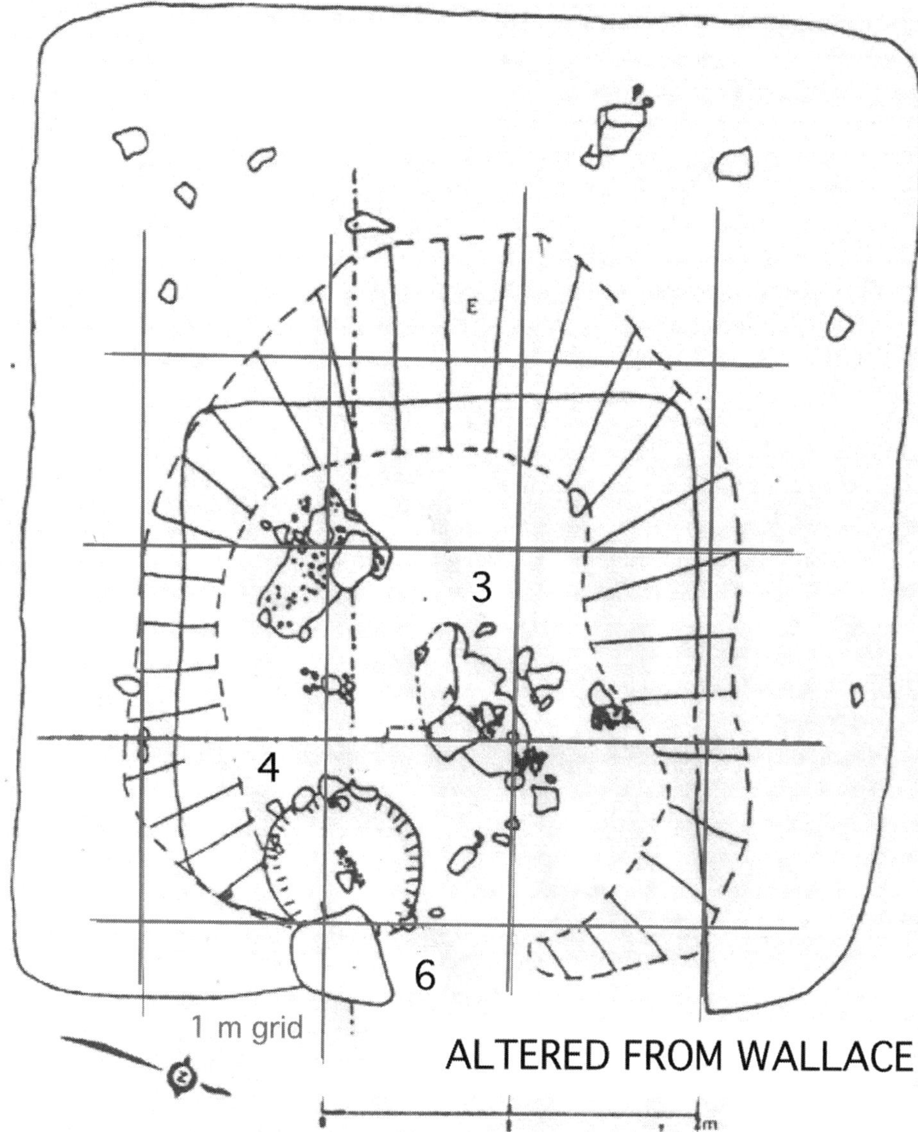

Figure 2: Archaeological features of the Furnace Hut at LAM. Courtesy Brigitta Wallace, 2008, used with permission. 3: Likely location of the furnace; 4: Shallow pit; 6: Large stone block

This working team is exclusive of the labor necessary to effectively operate the bellows. One of the objectives of this series was to eventually use only Viking Age-type equipment, with three of the experiments undertaken with human powered air. It is physically possible for two people (even one single operator) to conduct a successful iron smelt. Constant attention to the charcoal and ore additions to the furnace are required. If rising slag levels require a tapping or clearing of a blockage to the tuyere, extremely fast action is necessary. Cutting the airflow for any more than about five minutes will cause internal temperatures to drop, effectively "freezing" the liquid slag. Should this occur, it is almost impossible to regain the working dynamic inside the furnace. On many occasions, frantic activity is required!

It has been the experience of the author that the air volumes proposed by Sauder and Williams in 2002 are in fact necessary to create the same kind of dense, puck-like blooms known from Viking Age artifacts. This effective method calls for air volumes in the range of 1.2 to 1.5 liters per minute (LpM) per square centimeter of cross sectional area at tuyere level.[11] For a furnace in the size of those used in this series (tuyere area equals 380 cm^2), this computes to roughly 450 to 570 LpM. To produce air volumes in this range, a prototype smelting bellows on the Norse "double plate" layout had been built in 2008, which was used for this series.[12] Even with the large single plate size of roughly 30 by 65 cm and approximately a 40 cm loft, one full stroke would be required at least once per second. There were no precise measurements made of the effective air volumes produced by the test bellows throughout the experiments. In a set of static tests (bellows nozzle not attached to a furnace) made in Fall of 2008, this same unit was estimated to produce air volumes in the range of 600–700 LpM. In use within a working furnace system, the bellows was expected to have an effective delivery volume of considerably less than this. Air would be measured for the bellows equipped smelts at strokes per minute (SpM), recorded as an average. The strokes need to be as consistent as possible, over the entire 4–5 hour elapsed time of an individual smelt. To accomplish this, it was discovered that the most effective bellows team was comprised of a minimum of three (and better four) individuals, rotating into position about every 10 minutes.

Creating an Ore Analog

The source material used by the Norse at Vinland was a locally gathered primary bog iron ore. Unfortunately, there is no natural source for this type of ore within reasonable distance of the test location in Central Ontario. To that end, a separate project was mounted starting in 2008 to develop a workable "bog iron analog." A small sample of iron ore from the actual Norse occupation level at LAM had been supplied by Dr. Birgitta Wallace (from her 1973–76 excavations) for testing, as well as the information available in the Ingstad report from the initial excavations in the late 1960s.[13] Armed with this information, a mixture was formulated based on two commercially available iron oxide powders produced for use in potter's glazes. To this was added a small amount of silica sand (to promote slag formation) and whole wheat flour (to act as a binder). Hematite blasting grit was also used in combination for two of the experiments.

Table 1: Comparison of Oxides. "Slag Elements" are combined SiO2 and Al2O3

Material	Fe Oxide	Fe %	Slag Elements %
LAM—Ingstad	Fe2O3 + FeO	67.9	2.6
LAM—Wallace	Fe2O3	62.7	9.0
Red Oxide	Fe2O3	58.7	11.9
Black Oxide	Fe3O4	67.3	7.0
Hematite	Fe3O4	71.0	2.2
DD-1 (red)	Fe2O3	45.4	19.9
DD-2 (black)	Fe3O4	57.7	10.9

The materials were mixed dry, then water added to create a dough-like consistency. This was then spread in a layer about 1 cm thick on to metal sheets and allowed to dry in the sun. After several days, the resulting 'cookies' could be easily broken up into pieces roughly .5 to 2 cm in diameter. Thus both the relative chemistry and approximate physical size of the Norse ore could be simulated. There were at least three individual smelts undertaken in 2008 specifically to test the working properties of various mixtures: experiment 30 in March, 33 in April, and 36 in June.

Over the course of this series, a number of different mixtures of the two base analogs would be utilized. Only two samples were baked to determine the water content at point of use. This was the standard DD-2 mixture (Vinland 1, Vinland 3), which contained 8% and 9% water respectively. The higher value of 9% water was the variable used to correct the total ore values seen in table 2 (below).

In keeping with the archaeologist's estimates on the volumes of ore which might have been used originally at LAM, the total ore amounts for all the experiments were kept reasonably small. With between 18 to 20 kg ore added, the expectation was that the blooms produced should range between 3–5 kg.

Conducting an Effective Iron Smelt

The following additional aspects have proven critical in smelts by the author and other researchers:

- charcoal sized and screened between .5 to 2.5 cm diameter
- effective consumption rate between 8 and 12 minutes per "standard bucket" (about 1.8 kg) of charcoal
- ore additions start at 1 kg per charcoal bucket and are gradually increased to 2 kg
- ore is sprinkled evenly through each charcoal addition, not placed in thick layers
- the furnace is kept completely full (so constant additions of smaller amounts of charcoal required)
- slag taping is only undertaken if there is threat of blocking the tuyere flow
- availability of a standardized set of working tools

The charcoal used for all the experiments was standard 8 kg bags available at retail stores. It was a mix of hardwoods, maple, oak and hickory (depending on the supplier). The charcoal was normally processed by breaking it with wooden mallets through a heavy steel grid set with 2.5 cm gaps. This fell on to a second screen at roughly .5 cm. This allowed the finer particles and dust to be removed. For the final smelt at LAM, this equipment was not available. Instead, the larger pieces of charcoal were broken using mallets over wooden stumps. Then a similar sized fine screen was used to remove the dust and small fragments.

Extraction of the hot bloom was accomplished by drawing it out of the top of the furnace, a method the working team normally utilizes. Past experience has shown that this method generally results in less damage to the furnace itself. Once the last ore charge is added, an additional bucket measure of charcoal is added to ensure this last charge will remain completely covered. Then the furnace is allowed to burn down, a process that typically takes a further 30 minutes or so. Once the level drops to close to the tuyere, the air flow is reduced and the remaining burning charcoal, usually containing some partially reduced and loosely sintered iron fragments, is scooped out. This material is dumped to one side, ideally into buckets for safety reasons. The top of the slag bowl will be exposed, so the last scoops of charcoal usually contain runnels of liquid slag as well. At this point a heavy log "thumper" is used to hammer on the top of the white-hot bloom in place within the slag bowl. This serves both to slightly compress and, more importantly, loosen the bloom mass. Now a process of hooking and pulling on the bloom is used to completely free it from the slag bowl. The last step is to grab the bloom with a special set of oversized tongs.

The initial compaction of the bloom follows immediately. This process is best carried out by three workers, one holds the bloom, and two work over the surface with long handled sledges. Experience has shown the ideal working surface for this first step is actually not a hard anvil surface, but a plain wooden stub. (The irregular surface of the bloom will burn slightly into the wood, helping hold the mass in place.) The initial hammering should be carried out with very little force, as its purpose is to knock off any remaining slag, Looser pieces of mixed slag and partially sintered iron are also pushed in tightly against the primary mass. As the bloom "firms up" under the hammering, the power of the individual strokes can be increased to further drive off slag, weld in the surface, and compact internal voids. If possible, the bloom will be returned to the furnace, using the furnace as a kind of giant forge to bring the mass back up to the required working temperature. The ideal process is to use several heat and hammering cycles, eventually transferring over to a solid anvil surface. The last step would be to use a cutting wedge (historically an axe) to cut the compressed iron bloom into smaller working pieces.

Important to the function of these iron smelt events as experiments was the development and use of a standardized method of recording data. For the last "full historic" method smelt, this data was recorded by an isolated observer, but not communicated to the workers. A full photographic record was made of the progress of each smelt. On the day following an experiment, the debris fields were recorded for comparison to the work pattern and the archaeology at LAM.

The Experimental Series

Vinland One: June 2009 (Experiment 40)[14]

Objective: Test of furnace construction/workspace organization
Ore: 18 kg of DD-2 analog
Air: electric blower at 640 LpM
Tuyere: ceramic tube
Result: a dense planno-convex bloom at 4.9 kg (30% yield)

Description

For this first test in the series, the primary focus was on the size and wall material of the furnace itself. The basic Vinland 1 furnace was constructed with an ID at 20 cm, a total 65 cm tall. The walls were formed from straight clay, in this case roughly 5 cm thick. The end result of this construction was that the furnace developed some major cracks. These were stabilized by wrapping the furnace with fencing wire. There was no use of supporting stone slabs. This furnace was not equipped with a specific tapping arch. In operation the slag was found to run

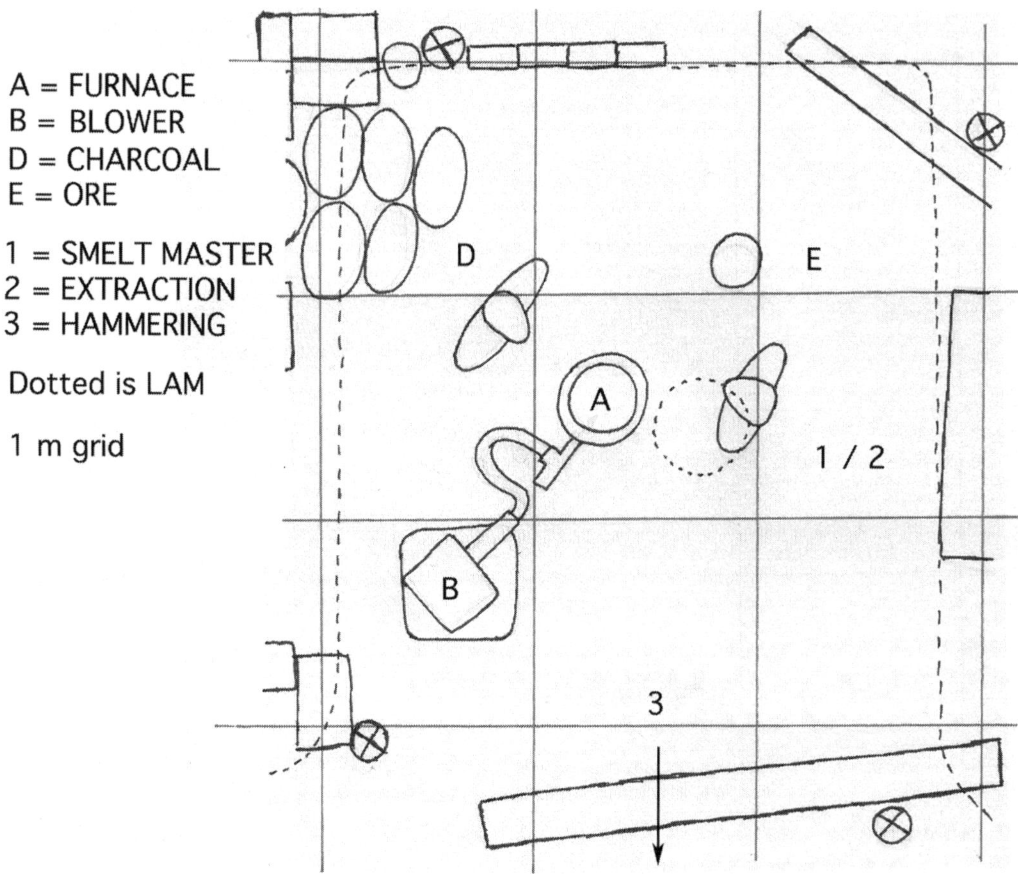

Figure 3: Work Layout—Vinland 1

"incontinent," with slag running from those same cracks in the walls. This is generally seen as an ideal situation, with the furnace "tapping itself" as slag levels rose inside. At this point, the fine details of equipment placement were not being explored. The LAM work area had been defined, with a layer of fresh sand placed over the entire work surface. The blower was set on a metal washtub that was placed roughly in the location of the pit feature in the archaeology. Charcoal was placed where it suited the workers best, not into the corner deemed most likely based on the archaeology. The stub used for compaction was one that had been installed for previous experiments, set outside the smelting area. Only two individuals made up the main work team, with a third keeping records.

The smelt proceeded as an almost textbook example of the process. The iron content of the ore, coupled by use of high air volumes, and inside a proven furnace layout, had suggested a good result. The bloom produced was a dense mass of soft iron, with a classic planno-convex shape.

In terms of size, shape and quality, it compared well to known Viking Age artifact blooms. The return yield of 30% was excellent, based on past smelts.

The use of a straight clay wall material, coupled with a fast construction to drying fire time, was expected to result in considerable wall cracking. This proved the case. The furnace performed extremely well, and it was felt that it easily could have could have been used for a second firing with very minimal repairs.

Vinland Two: October 2009 (Experiment #41)[15]

Objective: Box Bellows / learning sound indicators
Ore: 20.7 kg total mix of 6 kg DD-1/4.6 kg DD-2/10.1 kg Hematite
Air: mechanical box bellows with electric blower @ 800 LpM (estimated)
Tuyere: ceramic tube
Result: reasonably compact planno-convex bloom at 5.6 kg/30% yield

Description

An important step in eliminating modern elements to a smelt was learning to gauge the activity within the furnace by only human senses. Key to this was learning those indicators based on sound. The double plate style bellows intended for the final experiments in the series would create a variable, pulsing, air flow, quite different than the constant blast from the electric blower the working team was used to. An attempt to mimic this delivery flow, but still using mechanical power, was at the core of Vinland 2.

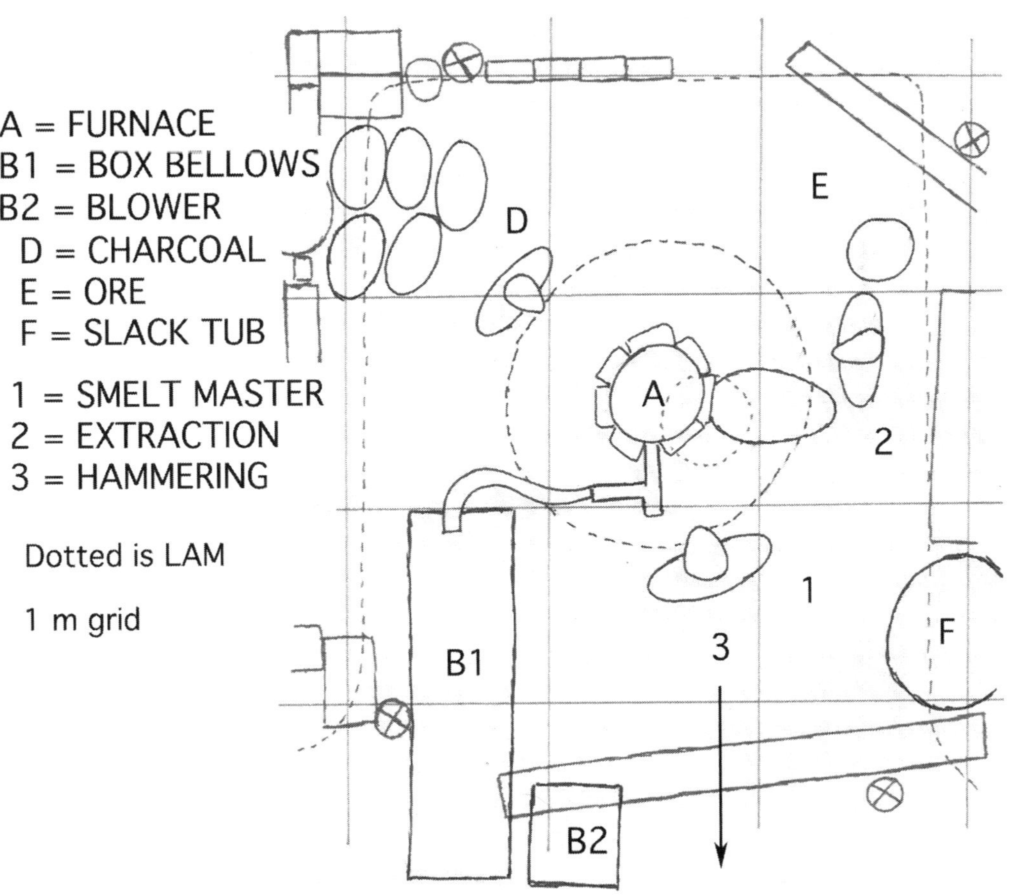

Figure 4: Work Layout—Vinland 2

Figure 5: The "Frankenbellows"—Vinland 2

To achieve this, a truly bizarre piece of equipment was constructed. The air delivery was in the form of a box bellows, which has an internal plate that shifts back and forth. As the plate moved, it would empty one chamber, while filling the other. Each side had a rectangular flap valve along the bottom edge to fill, and a standard one-way plumbing valve at the top to empty. The exhaust valves were linked in series to the hose running towards the tuyere. The mechanical problem was how to convert rotary power from an electric motor to reciprocating motion to move the bellows plate. This was accomplished by utilizing the rear running gear from a bicycle. A pulley shifted power from the motor to the rear wheel. The direction was such that the wheel would turn against the normal thrust of the gearing, driving the chain, in turn cranking the pedals. A rod with a pair of sliding joints allowed the rotation to be converted to the needed (more or less) straight thrust for the bellows plate. Although the derailer gear system did in fact allow for modifying input rotation speed to different pumping volumes, in practice only the very highest ratio was used. Once powered up, the whole assemblage would grind, quiver and clack—a very frightening machine.

The smelt pre-heat was started with this bellows system alone. Even though the machine was noisy, it did in fact produce a very visible and an audible pulsing of blast into the furnace. In the end it was found that the volume produced measured only about 250 LpM, not enough deemed necessary for a successful smelt. After about a half hour, the air system was quickly modified to allow attachment of the electric blower as well. Both systems would remain in place for the majority of the smelt, with the volume on the blower supplementing the volume from the box bellows. The effort expended on getting the box bellows machine correctly working seriously impacted the time available to construct the furnace itself. In fact the furnace was quickly and very roughly constructed the morning of the smelt, and not given the normal careful pre-heat cycle.

In the interests of time, the lower two layers of the furnace were constructed of slabs of wet clay, cut into rough "bricks" from commercially prepared clay blocks. Running out of prepared clay, the upper layer was constructed of regular firebricks. Wire was bound around this more or less octagonal structure, which in turn was supported by stone slabs with ash and sand mix packing the gaps. Extensive cracking and spalling off of the clay was expected—and was the case.

Again the combination of a good iron content in the ore plus larger air volumes was predicted to result in a high yield and good quality bloom. This was most certainly the case, this smelt producing the largest bloom in the whole series at 5.6 kg, another 30% yield. The bloom was again the classic planno-convex shape. When later sliced along the mid line, the lower portion of the bloom would been seen to have more void areas in it than that from Vinland 1.

Learning the auditory cues from a "pulsing" air system was not as instructional as might have been hoped. The additional air volume from the electric blower certainly was necessary, but this did reduce the effect of the box bellows airflow.

Vinland Three: November 2009 (Experiment #42)[16]

Objective: Use of bellows/placement of slack tub
Ore: 18 kg of DD–2 analog
Air: Norse-type "smelting" bellows at 72 SpM
Tuyere: steel pipe
Result: reasonably compact bloom at 2.9 kg/18% yield

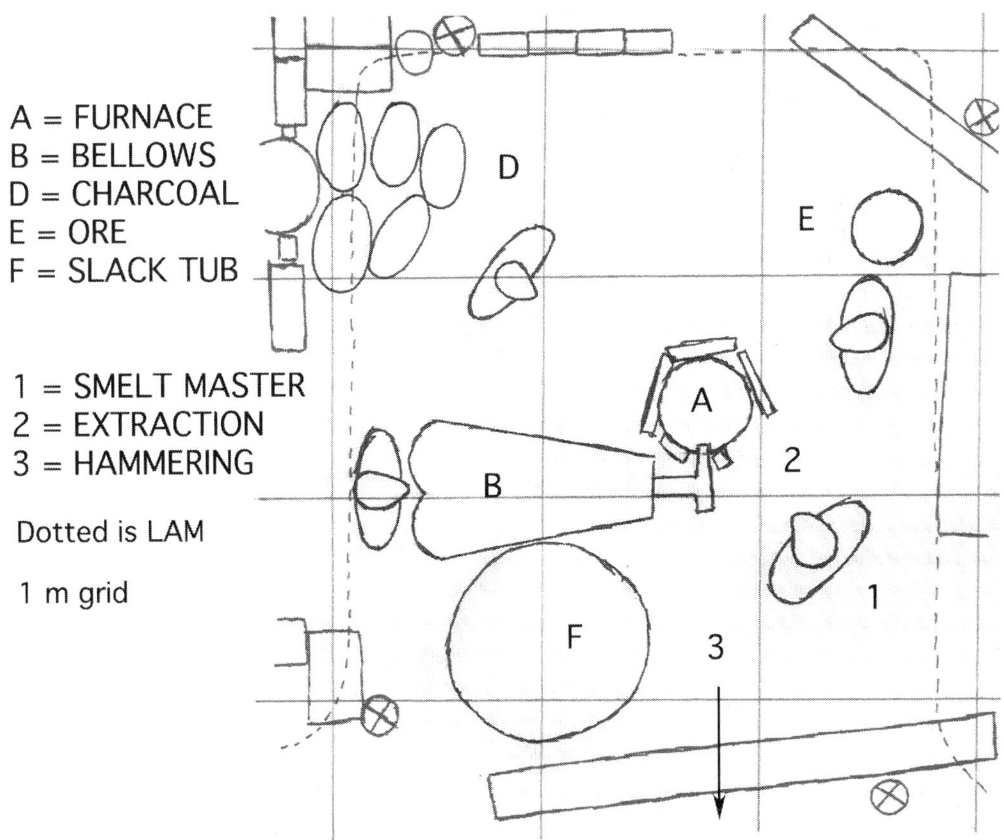

Figure 6: Work Layout—Vinland 3

Description

The most important step in the shift from a modern to more historic method was made with use of the human-powered bellows to provide all the air for this smelt. The primary working team did have earlier experience working differing bellows designs, but this was the first time this specific unit had been used for an entire smelting process. The bellows itself was mounted on a wooden frame that positioned the exhaust tube to roughly the correct height and angle to mount into the tuyere input. This also placed the operating handles at "roughly" the right position for comfortable use by the operator. In long-term use by several operators, "roughly" turned out to pose a problem. Within the working team, there was considerable difference in physical stature, running from about 172 to 188 cm, compounded by differing arm length proportions. It was discovered that individuals had quite different "styles" of bellows action. The variables were stroke length, speed, pressure and consistency. All can (and did) modify the exact effect of the blast into the furnace between individual operators.

One other significant change was in the physical layout of the equipment within the working space. One possible interpretation for the shallow pit found at the front left at LAM was that this was caused by a dug in wooden tub, filled with water for use as a cooling tub.[17] To duplicate this possible arrangement, a wooden half-barrel, roughly 80 cm in diameter, was placed in the indicated position. To provide for the angle between bellows tube and the tuyere, the bellows was then required to fit in tight between the furnace and the side wall. With the size of the bellows, the working space for the bellows operator was found to be too restrictive, especially for the larger individuals.

The furnace was constructed of the 50/50 clay and sand mixture suggested by the archaeology at LAM, with a steel pipe tuyere. Neither was expected to have much impact on the course of the smelt itself. Attachment of the bellows to the tuyere was made using the leather Y tube. In the smelt however, it was found that there was quickly significant erosion of the furnace wall at the tuyere. Eventually this caused a burn through of the wall material. Attempts were made to apply fresh clay and cover the area with sand mix. In the end it proved necessary to rush the extraction.

The bloom produced was considerably smaller, but reasonably compact and of good quality iron. A significant amount of reduced and partially sintered ore/iron was found mixed with the charcoal above the slag bowl and the developing bloom during the extraction phase. As much as 25% of the potentially available iron may have been lost. It was generally felt that the drop in air volume, and penetration into the furnace, caused by the shift to a human powered bellows was the cause of the lower yield.

In an attempt to spread working experience as wide as possible within the team, one of the less experienced workers undertook the extraction process. This resulted in significant damage to this furnace—enough that it could not possibly be used a second time.

Fully considered, there was absolutely no advantage to the placement of the slack tub as suggested by the pit feature, but many disadvantages.

Vinland Four: June 2010 (Experiment #43)[18]

Objective: All Viking Age tools AND methods/placement of anvil stub
Ore: 18 kg total mix of 10.3 kg DD-1/7.7 kg Hematite
Air: Norse type "smelting" bellows
Tuyere: steel pipe
Result: fragmented bloom at 1.9 kg/10% yield

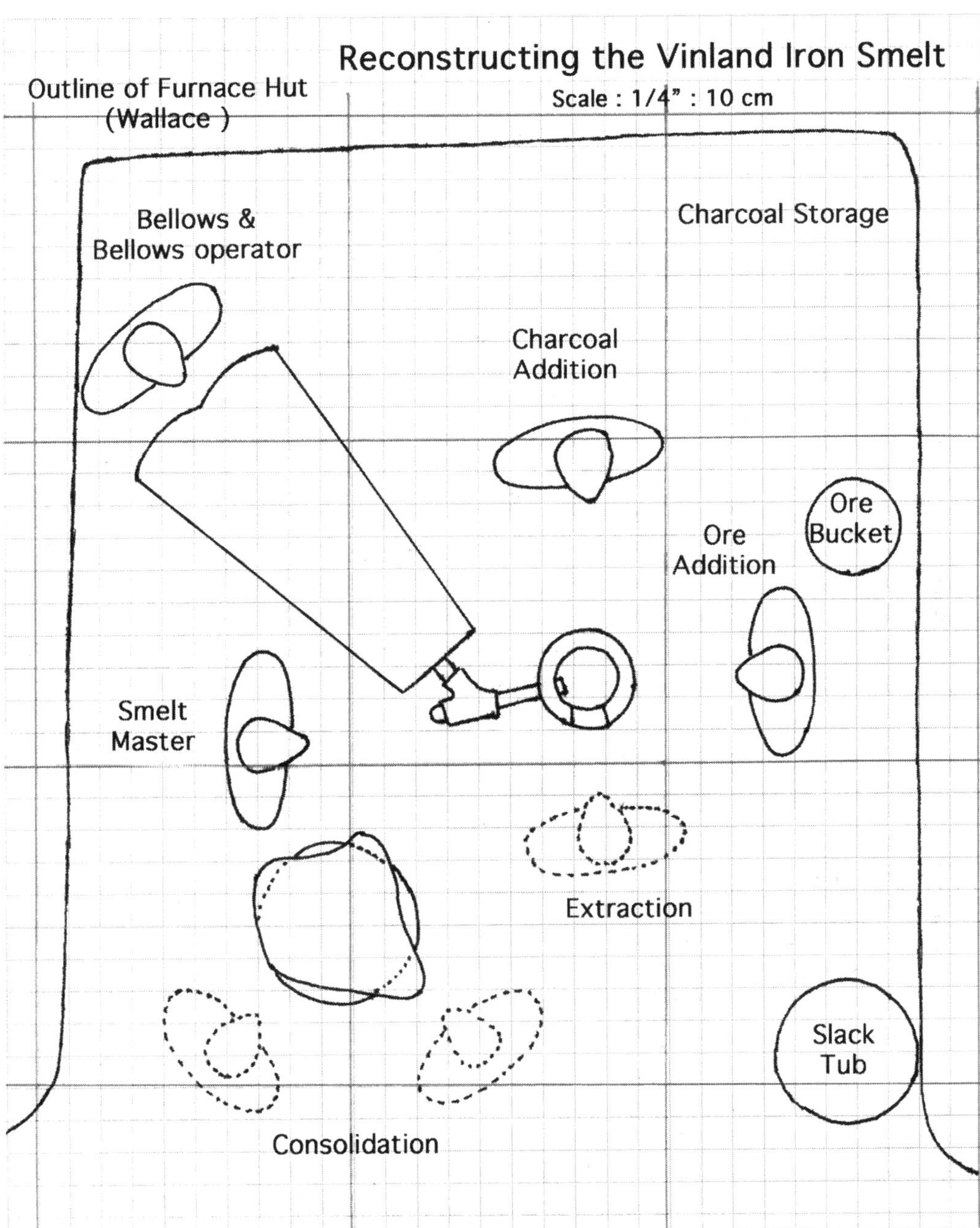

Figure 7: Work Layout—Vinland 4

Description

This experiment would determine the final placement of the various equipment. It was also a full dress rehearsal for the upcoming presentation for Parks Canada. As such, Viking Age period clothing was worn, and all historic type equipment and methods were employed. The only specifically modern element was the use of the required safety equipment (primarily eyewear).

The furnace construction was similar to that used in V3, clay and sand mix supported by stone slabs with a steel pipe tuyere. One change was slight shifting of the location of the tap arch and tuyere. In keeping with the LAM evidence, the tap arch was set pointing directly to the open end of the working space. The tuyere was placed roughly parallel to the line of the open end (entering at 90 degrees to the tap arch).

In place of the slack tub, a section of wooden timber was set into the ground to the left front. This was dug in to a depth of 40 cm, as indicated by the feature at LAM. More through luck than design, a large relatively flat-sided block of local limestone had been acquired. This was wedged up on the top of the stump to use as a stone anvil. The slack tub was shifted back to the extreme right of the open side. This location that made more practical sense to the working team.

The arrangement of the Y-tube meant that the bellows could now be placed in a diagonal line from the furnace, extending to the rear left corner of the working area. This would actually allow for more room for the operator. The position did create a bit of a bottleneck when new operators were rotated into position. In turn this shifted the best location for charcoal storage, into the right rear corner. This actually was more in keeping with suppositions made from the LAM evidence. The overall arrangement produced more space for working directly at the front of the furnace.

As an "all Norse" smelt, the working team had to rely on their own experience to make critical judgments about how the furnace was operating. With no clocks to guide them, bellows operators had to depend on their own sense of timing to attempt to maintain the correct air blast. (One member of the team, a musician, wrote a working chant to guide the pace.) Sound became one of the most important indicators of relative consumption and airflow. Maintaining constant amounts of charcoal and ore was accomplished through the use of standard measures, a wooden bucket and long handled metal scoop.

Unfortunately, a lack of available workers meant that the standard detailed recording was not made over the conduct of this smelt. The expectation was that with combination human-powered air and less precise regulation of sequencing, the overall yield from this smelt would be lower. This in fact proved to be the case, this bloom being the smallest of the entire series. The furnace would develop serious cracking, causing the loss via a self-tapping processes of large amounts of liquid slag. Primarily occurring near the end of the smelt sequence, the loss of slag also resulted in a significant drop in internal temperatures.

The process of compacting the bloom mass on a stone anvil represented a new experience for the team. The sound of striking was much different than what was expected. This was enough so that it was initially felt the metal produced was an undesirable high carbon cast iron. This proved not to be the case, but the final bloom was lumpy and not very well consolidated.

Vinland Five: August 2010 (Experiment #43)

Objective: Full demonstration at L'Anse aux Meadows HNSC
Ore: 20 kg of DD-2 analog
Air: Norse type "smelting" bellows at 93 SpM
Tuyere: steel pipe
Result: fragmented bloom at 2.8 kg/15% yield

Figure 8: Working area—Vinland 5

Description

The last smelt in the Vinland series took place inside the reconstructed Furnace Hut within the replica Viking Age compound at L'Anse aux Meadows NHSC itself. This smelt was more a duplication of experiment V4, but it was the public presentation of several years of effort. In many ways the working team was limited by many of the same restrictions that the original Norse iron-smelting group would have been. The only tools available were those that had been brought, and local materials had to be depended upon. It was known that there was a source of natural clay about 500 meters from the archaeological site. In the end, it was decided that the considerable extra work (and time) of preparing this raw clay would be avoided in favor of bringing a standard powdered clay to Newfoundland. Charcoal was purchased, although an attempt to make charcoal using ancient methods was undertaken as part of the demonstration program. The iron smelting team from Ontario would form the core of the workers, but many staff members from Parks Canada were involved as well. Mark Pilgrim of the Norse Encampment living history program would be guided through the role of smelt master.

Now the furnace was constructed inside a very flammable structure, with a wood pole roof and peat turf block walls. Although there was initially some concern about the potential of the roof catching on fire, these fears proved groundless. There are sparks created out the top of the furnace, mainly the result of burning charcoal dust. These are too small, however, to actually cause a problem. The extreme temperature of gasses voiding off the top of the furnace was quickly dispersed by the constant winds off the ocean side location.

The furnace was again the size, construction and placement suggested by the archaeology. Unlike earlier furnaces, there was no interior form used to stabilize the shape and control the size, which instead was determined by eye. The clay mixed initially proved far too soft, largely a result of rushing, too little attention, and considerable fatigue. Once the walls had been built up to a critical point, the entire construction slumped into itself. Fortunately, some fresh hands arrived just at the point of disaster. The clay was cleared away and re-mixed to a stiffer consistency and the build was repeated.

Once again the tuyere used was mild steel pipe. When the tuyere was set, this was also done by eye rather than with instruments. The result was measured after the fact and found to be slightly shallower, at 19 degrees down angle. The other equipment was placed much as they had been for V4. Charcoal would be broken using mallets over wooden stumps, but was then screened to remove dust. A test was made of tossing broken charcoal up off a tarp (cloak) to see if the wind would carry off the fines. This method, available to the Norse, did prove effective—if more difficult and time-consuming that shaking over metal screening in a box frame.

Once again, the details of the smelt would be recorded, but the workers themselves would have to rely on their own estimation of time. A better pool of enthusiastic labor was available, but few of the local staff had much experience with bellows operation. This was suspected to result in a certain unevenness in air delivery. In operation, the furnace would require a number of slag taps in its later stages, Again, there would be some cracking of the walls, but not as serious as V4 and venting was kept under control.

One serious problem did evolve as the bloom was pulled free from the furnace. The slag bowl had developed higher in the furnace, and so the bloom within it. In fact the bloom was positioned so that the steel tuyere had fused itself to the surface. When the bloom was pulled free, so came the tuyere, tearing free of the wall and ripping the furnace apart. Since this is always a moment of frantic activity, pieces of hot slag and furnace wall and burning charcoal were spread over a large area. Attention was concentrated at that point on the initial compaction of the bloom. Fast work was made with a shovel clearing away hot debris by a secondary team member. Although the initial size appeared good, it was obvious that the mass was quite fragmented internally. In the end the bloom would break into four pieces, at 1160, 640, 675, and 305 grams.

Conclusions

Table 2: Comparison of Results

Experiment	Ore Type	Ore KG	Fe %	Bloom KG	Yield %	Air
Norse	bog ore	18 ??	63.3	3 ?	17 ???	bellows
Vinland 1	DD-2	16.4	52.5	4.9	30	blower
Vinland 2	DD-1/DD-2/H	18.8	57.1	5.6	30	box/blower
Vinland 3	DD-2	16.4	52.5	2.9	18	bellows
Vinland 4	DD-1/H	16.4	52.8	1.6	10	bellows
Vinland 5	5 DD-2	18.2	52.5	2.8	15	bellows

1. Can a functional bloomery furnace be constructed and operated based on the evidence from LAM?

This experimental series shows that certainly this can be done. This furnace diameter, at roughly 20 cm, is on the small end of the effective range. It is still large enough that the relationship between heat loss over surface area to heat production due to volume does not impact negatively on the internal dynamics. Some efficiencies may be gained in a small furnace in terms of reducing overall charcoal consumption. As long as smaller blooms are the intended production, there is enough space available for both the mass to accumulate, and also for extraction to remain relatively simple. It is estimated that blooms much over 6 kg in total weight would completely fill the entire bottom of this size furnace, requiring complete dismantling of the furnace to remove them. Considering the relative ease of constructing such a small furnace, they easily could be considered "disposable" equipment.

Air flow has proven over many experiments to be the single most important factor in determining the overall quality of the metallic mass produced by a short shaft direct process bloomery furnace. With a smaller cross sectional area, the lower air volumes produced by Norse style bellows still allow for sufficient air to create a successful environment within the smelter.

The result is perhaps not the best quality, both in terms of size and density. The details of just what kind of air system them Norse would have had on hand in Vinland is unknown, and likely can never be stated for certain. Increasingly this has become a subject of interest to the author and this team, with research and experimentation continuing.

2. What is the most likely arrangement of working equipment within the confines dictated by the LAM "Furnace Hut"?

With the furnace centrally placed, and the most likely position of the tap arch/extraction towards the open front, the raw size of other equipment will determine its most probable placement. The large size of a bellows sufficient to provide the needed air volumes certainly limits the potential placement of this equipment. The most efficient placement is in a diagonal pointing from the left side of the furnace, then back towards the rear corner.

The pit feature uncovered at the left side of the buildings open end is suggested to be the remnants from a buried wooden stump. The 40 cm depth is about what is necessary to bury such a stump to provide the necessary stability. The wood would need to be carefully cut with axes to ensure it was flat enough and shaped closely to fit the anvil stone so it would remain fixed under repeated heavy hammer blows. This stump might not be carelessly discarded, and if pulled free of the ground, the surface would likely collapse into the kind of wide cylindrical profile seen in the archaeology. The fact that a large stone block was found up against this feature suggests that it was the actual stone anvil required for initial compaction of the still-hot bloom. It is proposed therefore that the working layout used for experiments V4 and V5 represents the most likely arrangement used at "Straumsforðr," at least for the primary smelting phase of iron production there.

3. Can a group of modern experimenters produce an iron bloom while working with Viking Age style equipment and methods?

The answer to this question is yes—but a qualified yes. Certainly the accumulated experience gathered over many years of smelting events proved absolutely invaluable. Despite what is commonly believed, successful iron smelting is tough work for the untrained or inexperienced. The ability to effectively judge what was happening inside the furnace through the changes in sound proved essential. Individual experiments let various members of the team take part managing the furnace through slag tapping and performing the final extraction of the bloom. There is no effective substitute for the experience of looking down the inside of a furnace and probing for a white-hot iron.

Some of the difference between individual blooms may be to variations within the various ore analog mixes. The relative iron contents only varied by roughly 10% however, while the yield numbers almost double. A significant improvement would have been expected in modern yields over the historic if a higher base iron content had been present in test ores. The sharp difference in yields between the use of modern air systems and historic types is obvious (see table 2).

The largest difficulty for the experimental team with the "All Norse" methods revolved around lack of experience working with the hand powered bellows. Maintaining a regular rhythm of strokes, and pressure of individual strokes, proved difficult for all operators. Attempting to match one individual's method to that of another was just beyond the workers. Consistency of air blast thus was not really attained, especially over the four-plus hours of a smelt.

A hand bellows is a much more subtle delivery system than an electric blower. A sharp snap of the wrist can instantly produce a sharp increase in delivery pressure, thus altering the penetration of the blast further into the furnace. Although this was theoretically understood, there was not enough accumulated experience in the bellows operators to produce that effect. Also any practical knowledge of how that application might affect the furnace in a desirable way remains unknown.

In the end however, this experimental series can be judged by what transpired at L'Anse aux Meadows NHSC on August 23, 2010. A furnace burned inside a replica of the Furnace Hut, about 200 meters from where Leif Eirikson's crew had built the original. Mark Pilgrim reached down inside a clay furnace and snatched out an iron bloom, about the same size as the first one created there, some 1000 years ago.

Acknowledgments

The experimental iron smelting series referred to in this paper was undertaken with the enthusiastic help of the Dark Ages Re-creation Company.

Establishing the methods for a successful smelt would have been impossible without the guidance, ideas and friendship of Lee Sauder, Skip Williams and Mike McCarthy.

A debt is owed to the gentle mentorship of Dr. Birgitta Wallace and Kevin Smith.

Thanks goes to McDonald's Home Hardware of Dundalk Ontario, who assisted with the cost of the charcoal used in these experiments.

The financial assistance of the Government of Ontario, through the Ontario Arts Council is gratefully acknowledged. Preparation of this paper, plus the costs of attending the 47th International Congress on Medieval Studies, was covered as part of a Crafts Projects Grant.

Working Teams

Along with the author, the following members of the Dark Ages Re-creation Company (and others) assisted with the individual smelt experiments:

Vinland 1: Ken Cook, Neil Peterson, ad Richard Schwitzer

Vinland 2: Ken Cook, Sam Falezone, Neil Peterson, and Richard Schwitzer

Vinland 3: Marcus Burnham, Ken Cook, Dave Cox, Sam Fallezone, Neil Peterson, and Steve Strang

Vinland 4: Ken Cook, Sam Falezone, and Pierre La Fountaine

Vinland 5: Ken Cook, Dave Cox, and Richard Schwitzer, and from Parks Canada, Meghan Arnott, Jessica Butler, Jake Hill, and Mark Pilgrim

Endnotes

1. Details on how the archaeological evidence from L'Anse aux Meadows was interpreted by the author is covered in Darrell Markewitz, "Iron Smelting in Vinland: Converting archaeological evidence to a practical method" (paper delivered at Forward Into the Past XX, Waterloo, ON, March 27, 2010. Available from http://www.warehamforge.ca/ironsmelting/LAM/Smelting-Vinland-V3.pdf, accessed April 6, 2014.
2. Darrell Markewitz, "Continuing Adventures In Early Iron: an Overview of Experimental Iron Smelts, 2001–2008," December 2008. (Revision of paper delivered at Friends of the Medieval Studies Society of the Royal Ontario Museum, 1st Annual Symposium, Toronto, March 25, 2006). Available from http://www.warehamforge.ca/ROMiron/V2/V2.html.
3. In this paper, the term "Norse" is defined as referring to the material culture of the Scandinavian peoples, both in the homelands and colonies across the North Atlantic, in the period of the "Viking Age," defined as 800–1050 CE.
4. See Anne Stine Ingstad, *The Discovery of a Norse Settlement in America*, trans. Elizabeth Seeberg (Irvington-on-Hudson, NY: Columbia University Press, 1977).
5. Birgitta Linderoth Wallace, *Westward Vikings: The Saga of L'Anse aux Meadows*(St John's, Newfoundland: Historic Sites Association of Newfoundland and Labrador in association with Parks Canada, 2006), 74.
6. Kristjan Eldjarn "IV Investigations," in Ingstad, 395.
7. Wallace, 62.
8. Lee Sauder, "Bloomery Construction" (unpublished manuscript, 2011).
9. Arne Espelund, "The Iron Story," (unpublished Parks Canada working document, 2001).
10. Ingstad, 211.
11. See Lee Sauder and Skip Williams, "A Practical Treatise on the Smelting and Smithing of Bloomery Iron," *Historical Metalurgy* 36:2 (2002): 128.
12. A problem long under consideration (and experimentation) by the author and his team is how to reliably produce these high volumes using Viking Age styled bellows. See Darrell Markewitz, "Bellows Reconstruction 3," January 28, 2008. http://warehamforgeblog.blogspot.com/2008/01/bellows-reonstruction–3.html, and "Air Delivery Test—Norse Smelting Bellows," November 14, 2008.
13. Anna Rosenqvist, "Material Investigations," in Ingstad, 396.
14. Darrell Markewitz, "Vinland 1: Working Towards a Reconstruction of a L'Anse aux Meadows Smelt" 2009, http://www.warehamforge.ca/ironsmelting/LAM/LAM-one/report05–09.html.
15. Darrell Markewitz, "Vinland 2: Working Towards a Reconstruction of a L'Anse aux Meadows Smelt," 2009, http://www.warehamforge.ca/ironsmelting/LAM/Vinland2/report10–09.html.

16. Darrell Markewitz, "Vinland 3: Working towards a reconstruction of the L'Anse aux Meadows Smelt," 2009, http://www.warehamforge.ca/ironsmelting/LAM/Vinland3/report11–09.html.
17. Birgitta Wallace, statement made during round table discussions at "Iron Processing at L'Anse aux Meadows," Parks Canada workshop, June 2001, from the author's notes.
18. Darrell Markewitz, "Vinland 3: Working towards a reconstruction of the L'Anse aux Meadows Smelt," 2010, http://www.warehamforge.ca/ironsmelting/LAM/Vinland4/report6-10.html22; Darrell Markewitz, "Smelting at Vinland—draft report," 2010, http://warehamforgeblog.blogspot.ca/2010/09/smelting-in-vinland-draft-report.html.

THE CHIVALRIC WARRIOR AS MAN OF HIS WORD

Steven Muhlberger

Let's start with a story about Boucicaut the Younger. Boucicaut, or properly Jehan le Maingre, was the son of a Marshal of France and was appointed Marshal himself in 1391, at the age of 25. As Marshal, he took part in several major campaigns, including the disastrous crusade of Nicopolis and the disastrous defeat at Agincourt. But his early career was noteworthy for his participation in a number of flashy deeds of arms, what I sometimes call *formal* combats or deeds of arms, or simply challenges. Here's one of them, one which did not come off, but which we are told nevertheless reflected credit on Boucicaut and the reverse on his English opponent.[1]

> *The duke of Bourbon and Boucicaut] passed through the county of Foix. There Boucicaut often found himself in the company of Englishmen, and they ate and drank together as the occasion offered itself... Those Englishmen noticed some abstinences that Messire Boucicaut was practicing. They asked if this had anything to do with fighting; and if it did, he would soon find someone to release him from [that vow]. Boucicaut replied to them that in truth these abstinences indicated willingness to fight to extremity... They went so far with these discussions that an English lord of the country, named the lord of Chastiauneuf, and who was a relative of the said count of Foix, accepted [an] engagement [of] twenty against twenty, and that he would be the chief of the English, and Messire Boucicaut of the French.*
>
> *So it was agreed by the two parties, and it was given to Boucicaut to seek a judge... But I do not know if the English found in [his candidates] their excuse to abandon the affair, and whether they repented of this undertaking, for they did not wish to accept as judges either the duke of Bourbon or many others whom Messire Boucicaut presented. When Messire Boucicaut saw that, it much weighed upon him, because he saw very well that they already had repented of it. Because he wished above all to perform the combat, in order that they should not be able to excuse themselves from it, and not know what more to say, he offered to them that the battle should be before the count of Foix, but the said count did not at all wish to accept or secure the field of combat for them. So the affair remained to the great honor of Boucicaut.*

"So the affair remained to the great honor of Boucicaut." Why does the author of this tale—who was an anonymous biographer of Boucicaut writing circa 1409—think Boucicaut won honor here? Here's the title he gives to this story:

> *How Messire Bouciquaut went to Spain, and how, on his return, Chastiauneuf, an English lord, undertook a deed of arms with him... And then did not wish it or did not dare to stand by it.*[2]

Chivalric literature of the later Middle Ages often includes accounts of formal deeds of arms, in which the weapons used, the number of blows to be delivered or jousting courses to be run, and other aspects of the combat were carefully regulated. The descriptions of such combats focus on how well the opponents fulfilled those stated conditions.

It will be my argument in this paper that men like Boucicaut, who took part in formal deeds so that they might win honor (a word that combined the notions of fame and respect as well as the modern one of honor), such men attached an overwhelming importance to being seen as men of their word. Depictions of Anglo-French and Iberian challenges in the late fourteenth and early fifteenth centuries give us stories of men like Boucicaut who, once committed to a course of action, did not back down. They won honor at the expense of those who "did not dare to stand by" their word.

That of course is not amazing finding, and if that's all I had to say, I wouldn't waste your time. What interests me, however, is this. Warriors seeking honor in formal combats were so attached to this notion of standing by their word, that their behavior produced or supported a literary motif which we might call "the angry champion." The angry champion was a man who lost his cool when he felt that someone had prevented him from performing his deed precisely as had been earlier agreed. Literary depictions of this anger indicate how strongly such men desired to be able to say they had done what they said they would do. The touchiness of these champions when put in what they saw as a false position helps us re-imagine one aspect of the emotional life of the fighting aristocracy.

We can understand why warriors were such sticklers on these occasions if we realize that a commitment to perform defined deed was understood as a contract or even a vow, which it would be sinful or at least disgraceful to leave unfulfilled. A common term for a deed of arms, whether a formal deed in the lists or a deed of war, was *emprise*, an enterprise that obliged members of a group to accomplish a set undertaking. In 1351, Geoffroi de Charny defined a typical joust in these terms:

> *An emprise for jousting is announced for a certain place on a certain day to deliver all knights of three lances and not more, and nothing else is announced except the prize.*

This definition is the basis for Charny's discussion of what the law of arms required jousters to do. It is fairly obvious what the defenders (whom we can call "sharers in the *emprise*") are committing themselves to do. But note that the knights who are coming to the joust also make a commitment. They have obliged themselves to run courses or lances against the defenders, and the defenders are delivering them of that obligation. In other words, all the jousters have undertaken a clearly defined, formal, legal obligation, and are looking to be released from it. They are delivered or released not because they have been excused that debt, but because they have paid it.

We can also see formal deeds of arms as the working out of vows, with all the solemnity that goes with vows. The terms "vow" and "emprise" were sometimes equated.[3] Vowing to accomplish a martial deed had a long history by the later Middle Ages. Think of the crusader vow. More relevantly, since it was an oath taken by warriors in front of warriors, recall the famous Vow of the Pheasant taken by Philip the Good, Duke of Burgundy and his guests at a feast in 1454 to undertake an expedition to Constantinople. This was by no means the first chivalric vow on a bird. These vows, despite their peculiar format, were taken quite seriously.[4]

We can now appreciate how the angry champion might emerge when his ability to fulfill his vow was frustrated. Let's look at a couple of angry champions from the pages of Froissart.

The first of these is Sir Peter de Courtenay, an Englishman who in the late 1380s fought a French champion in Paris before King Charles and his court.[5] Precisely what terms of combat had been agreed to is not said, but whatever they were, the king halted the deed after a single course of jousting. One suspects that this was done because the French champion seemed to be losing. Froissart says "The king would not suffer more to be done, to the great discontent of the English knight, who seemed desirous of pushing the combat to extremities." The French lords tried their best to avoid an unfortunate scene:

> *[Courtenay] was… appeased by fair speeches, saying, he ought to be satisfied, for he had done enough; and he was presented with very rich gifts by the king and the Duke of Burgundy.*[6]

But in fact, Courtenay was *not* satisfied. As he rode back to Calais he needed only an opportunity to let his dissatisfaction to burst out. When the Countess of St. Pol, an Englishwoman, asked him what he thought of his reception by the lords of France, he replied:

> *To be sure, madam, I am perfectly contented as to the reception I have had; but, in regard to the reason I crossed the sea, they have but shabbily acquitted themselves: …if a knight of France had come to England, and challenged any one, however high his rank, it would have been accepted, and the terms faithfully fulfilled to his utmost pleasure; but this has been* ***refused*** *me.… when we had run one course with the lance, I was stopped, and ordered from the king to attempt nothing more, for that we had done enough. I therefore say, madam, and shall say and maintain it wherever I go, that I have not met any one able to oppose me in arms; and that it has not been my fault, but rests solely with the knights of France.*[7]

The Frenchmen who heard about this were very offended, as one might expect. But as Froissart presents Courtenay's point of view it seems not so much a matter of the English champion bragging about his skill or casting doubt on the abilities of the French—though that may be there—as it is a matter of Courtenay angrily insisting that it was *not his fault* that he did not fulfill the terms of the encounter. He is angry that someone might look at the situation and blame him for not doing what he said he would do. It is this possibility that makes him say, after some pro forma courtesy, that he has been shabbily treated.

Two more angry champions from the pages of Froissart are to be found in his report of the famous deed of arms which took place in 1381 at Vannes in Brittany at the end of an unsuccessful campaign led by the Earl of Buckingham. In two cases Froissart shows English champions on the verge of defeat by Frenchmen being forced by their countrymen to withdraw from the contest. The Frenchmen did not gloat about their superiority;[8] rather, they are shown to be angry. The Bastard Clarins, the first of these French champions, was surprised and upset by this default and told the English so, holding them collectively responsible for letting him down: "Lords," he said, "you do me wrong, and since you don't want Edward [their champion] to do any more, give me someone else with whom I can complete my *armes*." The earl had to admit that this was a legitimate demand, and another opponent was supplied. Later, a similar scene was enacted when Jean de Châteaumorand was getting the best of Jannekin Clinton, a trusted squire of the Earl of Buckingham. Again, the earl forced his retainer to withdraw. Châteaumorand found himself in precisely the same position that the Bastard Clarins had been in shortly before. His deeds of arms unfulfilled, he felt compelled to protest: "You *do me wrong and a shameful injury* if I leave here without performing the deed of arms." And again, he had to be provided with an opponent who would go the course with him.

Froissart, one may object, may not be the best source of information for this matter. He was after all very inventive and some of his stories, for instance his long account of the jousts at St. Inglevert, have undoubtedly been fictionalized. Yet we have other evidence that portrays angry champions similarly objecting to their treatment. One of the best depictions of a large formal joust, the Spanish *Passo Honroso,* shows us much the same dynamic at work in Léon in 1434.

The *Passo Honroso* was a grand, month-long event hosted and designed by one Suero de Quiñones, who also played the starring role on the field.[9] It was his *emprise* that constituted the rules of the joust and committed him and nine other knights to run courses against all comers until three spears were broken. But despite the fact that Suero was the patron of the joust, partway through he found himself in conflict with the judges, and the issue was whether he could fulfill an additional commitment. He showed up in the lists wearing three pieces of armor less than a full kit: no visor, no left pauldron, and no plackart. Suero claimed that he had made a public challenge to fight like this and had to be allowed to do it. The judges, after consulting with each other, declared that fighting in this dangerous condition went well beyond the rules which they were authorized to enforce, and forbade Suero to fight without full armor; indeed, the judges seized his reins and put him under arrest, to be held in his pavilion for the rest of the day. Suero defied them, saying "that they were doing him a great injustice and injury, since he had made a promise, as he had said, they should allow him to fulfill his vow and promise [*boto e promesa*]." The judges were unmoved and were as determined as Suero, and ordered their heralds to take him to the pavilion. Suero appealed to the heralds and other officials of the joust to witness "as to the means and way in which he had come there to fulfill what he had promised [and the rest of what had happened]." As he was led away, Suero did tell the judges "that he would obey their order, since he had promised to do so" but tempers continued to run high. The retreating Suero was being serenaded by trumpeters and minstrels; the judges told them to stop or they too would be arrested. Later on, after getting another message from Suero asking permission to run another non-standard joust, the judges "took such great umbrage" that they refused to let any further jousting to take place, "because that day they were vexed, to such an extent that they could not properly watch deeds of arms that day, nor would they allow it."[10]

I have cited this incident at length because it is amusing, but also because it is instructive. The account of the *Passo Honroso* seems to me to be in some ways more reliable than Froissart's account of Vannes, or Courtney's joust at Paris, or the joust of St. Inglevert; for one thing, there is no hint that Froissart attended any of those deeds, while the recorder of the *Passo,* Pero Rodríguez de Lena, was an eyewitness commissioned by Suero to keep a careful record of every course. (And careful it is.) Nonetheless, the stated concerns of the angry champions are very much the same in Froissart, in Rodrígeuz de Lena, and in other accounts such as the anonymous verse account of St. Inglevert, where an English knight abuses the joust's officials for trying to cheat him of a promised course.

The angry champion dynamic springs in part from contradictory elements in the evaluation of how well a competitor was seen to do in a joust. By the second half of the 15th century jousting was being evaluated on a point system, quite like most sports are today, and it was often possible to say unambiguously who had won and who had lost. In the earlier period we are talking about, evaluation was much more subjective. We can see this in both Froissart's account of St. Inglevert, and Rodríguez de Lena's precise record of the *Passo Honroso*. It is quite common in Froissart for it to be stated that both competitors had done well—no winner, no loser. Rodríguez de Lena usually has an opinion as to which jouster did better in a given set of courses, but it is a matter of a practiced observer making a judgment call. It is quite possible that other observers had different opinions.

But of course, even if matters of victory and defeat were sometimes downplayed in the friendlier competitions, medieval knights wanted to excel. To paraphrase Charny, they wanted to be the one who was worth more because he did more. A competitor might achieve this in a joust by unhorsing his opponent—that was pretty unambiguous—or by knocking him down in a foot combat. But it was perhaps more possible to show what one was made of by making a commitment and following through. The significance of the commitment and the risks involved should not be underestimated. Ignore for the moment the physical dangers and the physical courage that participating required. Taking part in a formal combat involved other risks. One might be humiliated before one's enemies and even worse before one's friends. To have it said that one had not fulfilled one's *emprise* might be a terrible fate. It would reflect on one's worth as a man at arms.

The need for a man at arms, a respectable warrior of standing, to establish a reputation as a man of his word was a powerful one. An awareness of evaluating eyes and critical tongues was the force that sometimes brought competitors into conflict with the judges and the great lords who sponsored and regulated the events. The sponsors had a different set of priorities, including a desire to be seen as patrons of chivalry by friend and foe alike. One purpose of the rules regulating such events was to avoid injury or death if at all possible, and to keep things friendly. Formal chivalric competition was meant to take place within limits; the violence was supposed to be contained. For instance, King Charles, when he stopped Courtney from finishing his *emprise* in Paris, was no doubt thinking of how terrible it would be if the French champion was defeated right before him. Prestige was at stake. But also there was the terrible possibility that one of the rivals would be seriously injured, which might have disrupted the fragile truce that obtained between France and England at that moment. For another instance, the judges at the *Passo Honroso* seem to have felt that their power came ultimately from the King of Castile, who would not approve of Suero's crazy, dangerous and showoffy challenge if somebody got hurt. Perhaps with some exaggeration, they said they risked "losing our honor and our heads." Keeping the lid on a formal deed of arms, especially one between habitual rivals, was no easy matter. That was why no one was particularly interested in serving as the judge or patron of Boucicaut's proposed battle of 20 against 20, with which we opened the paper. It seemed a thankless task, in which the umpire might lose more than he could gain. But the prudence of the judge, a necessary part of his duty and role, could not help but seem infuriating to competitors determined to show their worth.

Thus, the anger of the angry champion. But what about his fear? There seems to be a fear behind the anger, which fear seems to spring from anticipation of criticism that might seem all too close to charges of cowardice. By entering on an emprise or a vow, the competitor was posing a vital question: When he committed himself to performing a certain act, a dangerous deed of arms, would others believe that he would follow through? The anger of a man who felt he had been cheated of the opportunity to show that he was reliable indicates how important it was for a chivalric warrior to be seen as a man of his word.

Endnotes

1. *Le Livre des fais du bon Messire Jehan le Maingre dit Bouciquaut...*, ed. Denis Lalande (Geneva: Librairie Droz, 1985) 57–8; Chastiauneuf was a Gascon of English allegiance.
2. *Livre des fais*, 56.
3. The Duke of Bourbon's 1415 charter for his chivalric order states the members have *voué et emprins* various obligations: *Choix de pieces inédites relatives au règne de Charles VI,* ed L. Douët d'Arcq, 10 vols. (Paris: SHF, 1863), 1:370. There is also the famous vow of James Audley to be the foremost in the attack if he were ever in a major battle, which vow he fulfilled at Poitiers; Jean Froissart, *Oeuvres,* ed. Kervyn de Lettenhove. 25 vols. (Brussels, 1867–77) [hereafter KL] 5:436–7.
4. Steven Muhlberger, *Deeds of Arms: Formal combats in the late fourteenth century* (Highland Village, TX: Chivalry Bookshelf, 2005), 42–3.
5. Muhlberger, 170–80 for the charged and complex political background; Courtenay and his French opponent represented the war parties of their kingdoms, and their deed of arms was a replay of a recent campaign in Flanders.
6. KL 14: 44; Jean Froissart, *Chronicles,* trans. Thomas Johnes. 2 vols. (London, 1862) [hereafter Johnes], 2:411.
7. KL 14: 45; Johnes, 2:412
8. Compare to a later account derived from Châteaumorand, which focuses on how much damage the French champions inflicted on the English. *La Chronique du bon duc Loys de Bourbon,* ed. A.M. Chazaud (Paris: Renouard, 1876), 128–35.
9. Noel Fallows, *Jousting in Medieval and Renaissance Iberia* (Woodbridge: Boydell Press, 2010) includes long excerpts of Pero Rodríguez de Lena's account and a translation on pp. 399–501.
10. Fallows, 442–6

"SEEKING THAT WHICH CANNOT BE FOUND": THE USE OF LANCELOT THROUGH PRECURSOR TEXTS AS CONTEMPORARY SOCIAL COMMENTARY IN *THE ONCE AND FUTURE KING*

Emerson Storm Fillman Richards

In the wake of his (now lost) thesis on Thomas Malory at Queen's College of Cambridge University in the late 1920s, Terence Hanbury White was poised to remark upon the different representations of chivalry in historical literatures. White's tetralogy, *The Once and Future King* (1958), demonstrates his knowledge of the Arthurian tradition and related elements of medieval culture. I propose that through the precursor texts figured in White's work we can discern his responses to various pressing political (and, for White, personal) concerns of early twentieth century England; chief among these interests was the imminence of World War II.[1] I focus on two Lancelot-related examples to suggest that White's aggregate of precursor texts is not a superficial pastiche of textual and cultural references, but a calculated selection of allusions to critique this and other contemporary issues in a sophisticated way.

The Once and Future King[2] is the common title of the compiled tetralogy of books by T. H. White published in 1958. Three of the books had been published individually prior to 1958. Episodes from *The Sword in the Stone* (1939) were deleted for the 1958 publication. The second book, *The Queen of Air and Darkness*, originally published in 1939 as *The Witch in the Wood*, underwent the most drastic changes before appearing in *OFK*. *The Ill-Made Knight* (1940) was mostly unchanged, and *The Candle in the Wind*, written in 1941, had not appeared in print before 1958. White intended a fifth volume, *The Book of Merlyn*, should be published as a conclusion to *OFK*,[3] but it was rejected by the publisher. *Merlyn* was posthumously published after revision and reorganizing.

When he began writing *SS*, White wrote to his mentor, Leonard James Potts, on 14 January 1938, expressing his confusion about whether he was writing a children's book, or a more serious work.[4] To those without a background in medieval literature, the narrative of *SS*, detailing Arthur's adolescence, may seem a charming, if complex, story of "all things lost and wonderful and sad" (as the jacket blurb of a 1987 paperback edition heralds), pertaining chiefly to the novel's primary audience, children and young adolescents. But there is more going here. Heather Worthington's article on the tetralogy, "From Children's Story to Adult Fiction: T. H. White's *The Once and Future King*," considers the biographic-style of the novels using the lens of White's vexed portrayal of women. She defends White's stylistic choices that place him in the not entirely accurate genre of Young Adult Fiction: As Arthur matures, she observes, so do White's tone and style as he considers the more mature themes with which Arthur will have to cope—Worthington explains,"[t]he narrative structure which takes Arthur from childhood to maturity is paralleled in the textual structure" of the novels.[5] Both *QAD* and *WW* conclude with a discourse on Arthur's sin of incest and the imperative fall he will suffer, and White primes the reader to turn from talking animals and tutorage by saints and wizards in the first two books toward the darker themes of incest, adultery, aging, and the destruction of Camelot of the second two books. The two books following *QAD* show "a closer adherence to the original tale penned by Malory,"[6] as well as a closer adherence to Malory's own sources, which include much of the French tradition.

If we consider references to the canon of chivalric literature embedded in White's tetralogy, his representation of the canon and its argument becomes increasingly nuanced as *OFK* progresses. To demonstrate this, I will focus on White's representations of Lancelot, chiefly his reappropriations of five medieval sources: the late 12th century *Roman de Rou* by Wace and the contemporary *Yvain: ou le chevalier au lion* by Chrétien de Troyes, the early thirteenth century *La Quête du Saint Graal* from the Vulgate Cycle, *Songe d'Helain, d'Hector, et de Gaivain* of the Post-Vulgate Cycle and the Sir Gawain chapter of Malory's *The Tale of the Sankgreal Briefly Drawn out of French Which is A Tale Chronicled For One of the Truest and One of the Holiest That is in This World.*[7] I will then explicate White's use of Lancelot to critique chivalric codes. Since White's work is informed by (at least some) consideration of primary texts (as documented by letters to his mentor) tracing certain cultural traditions, such as the nature of chivalry, through his books proves more valuable than using the works of other modern authors who may not have considered the antecedent texts.

My critical models are source criticism and adaptation theory. Much work has been done on source criticism relating to White's contemporary, J. R. R. Tolkien. Since appreciably less scholarly work has been done on White's books, it is not surprising that there is much less source criticism dealing specifically with his corpus. So, to some extent, Tolkienian source criticism will guide my reading of White and his sources. Source criticism, however, is a controversial field in which "there has been too little understanding of the proper scope, limits, and methodology of successful source study, leading to many poor examples."[8] I will follow the methodology and criteria set out by Jason Fisher and E. L. Risden in *Tolkien and the Study of his Sources.* Scholars question whether it is enough to be "satisfied with the soup that is set up before us"—that is "the story as it is served up by its author"—and to not desire "to see the bones of the ox out of which it has been boiled."[9] Fisher's essay encourages those who engage with source criticism to "not simply point out that an author incorporates this or that source, but to try to explain *why* he might have done so."[10] In "Genesis of a Medieval Book," C. S. Lewis reminds his modern audience that "[t]he scholar's ideal of accuracy in translation, the historian's ideal of fidelity to a document and the artist's ideal of originality, are all alike absent from the minds of [medieval authors]... They seem to be enslaved to their originals...[but] they do not hesitate to supplement them from their own knowledge and, still more, from their own imagination."[11] Medieval authors "freely modified and adapted [their sources] to their own purposes, to the demands of their selected form and to the needs of their time."[12] With this in mind, derivative elements in the works of Tolkien[13] and White, authors whose subject matter was medieval or pseudo-medieval, seem more in line with their motive and less as though the authors lacked originality. Risden's essay summarizes much of the previous scholarship in general source criticism. He enumerates Harold Bloom's "six patterns" of poetic influence or poetic revision in *The Anxiety of*

Influence. Of Bloom's six definitions, the patterns that best apply to White's interpretation of the Arthuriad are:

> ...2. *Tessera*, ... *A poet antithetically "completes" his precursor, by so reading the parent-poem as to retain its terms but to mean them in another sense, as though the precursor has failed to go far enough....*
>
> 4. *Daemonization*, ... *The later poet opens himself to what he believes to be a power in the parent-poem that does not belong to the parent proper, but to a range of being just beyond that precursor. He does this, in his poem, by stationing its relation to the parent-poem as to generalize away the uniqueness of the earlier work....*
>
> 5. *Askesis, or a movement of self-purgation which intends to attainment of a state of solitude...[the poet] yields up part of his own human and imaginative endowment, so as to separate himself from others, including his precursor...*[14]

Risden uses these paradigms to "consider...[the] critical method as we compare related texts."[15] The way in which the Arthurian legend has been transmitted since its inception lends itself easily to being categorized as *tessera*. The author adds or omits his or her own culturally- or personally-driven detail, shifting the emphasis of the revision from the source legend or legends. In this respect, the Arthurian legend is very unstable—rarely does a character retain fixed characteristics or the narrative follow well-rehearsed plots.[16] Though it originates in Wales, the Arthurian tradition does not belong to one nation or group. Arthurian references and cycles became native to countries across Europe in the Middle Ages, and across the world in modern times. If we consider the variations of the legend after the Vulgate Cycle,[17] in conjunction with White's claim that "the whole Arthurian story is a regular Greek doom, comparable to that of *Orestes*"[18] (by this, White most likely refers to *The Orestia*, not the play *Orestes*) and the comparison of the legend to an Aristotelian tragedy in *QAD*, then we can see more clearly White's archetypal consideration of Arthuriana emerge. By defining the various archetypes embedded within the Arthurian legend and adding to them, White submits his work to Bloom's pattern of *daemonization*. White did not adhere to a strict representation of medieval Arthurian legend; he allowed his representations of characters and narratives to be influenced not only by many precursor works but also his idiom and psyche; as he observes of the Lancelot character, his version of the knight reflects his own flaws.[19] Because of similar additions to precursor material, the narrative can also be considered *askesis*. Risden suggests that critics benefit from understanding the type of influence used by an author.[20]

More than recognizing that there *is* influence of precursor texts, source criticism is a viable approach to White's novels in that it "combines... elements of historicism, biographical criticism and philology to determine how other works have somehow directed the course of those one is seeking to elucidate."[21] While the critical work on adaptation theory by Lawerence Venuti does not address medieval texts, his methodology and consideration of *what adaptation is* can be applied to medieval texts. Because of the recycling of plots, characters and chunks of text, medieval literature is rife with adaptations of prior literary sources. The Arthurian legend is no exception. Venuti's observations on the hermeneutic logic of adaptation is particularly relevant to White's case:

> *[t]he relation between such second-order creations and their source materials is not communicative but hermeneutic... The hermeneutic relation can be seen not only as interpretive, fixing the form and meaning of the source materials, but as interrogative, exposing the cultural and social conditions of those materials and of the translation or adaptation that has processed them.*[22]

When read alongside Bloom's *Anxiety of Influence,* Venuti suggests that adaptations do not merely represent the Bloomian category of *clinamen* (fixative, corrective), but rather, by understanding the role of the adaptor, the scholar can better understand the culture and society to which the adapter belonged. White does not seek to "fix" Arthurian legend. Instead, he suggests an understanding of the culture around the Arthuriad and chivalry by relating it to a contemporary audience. We may thus discern elements in his version of Arthur that are "not only... interpretive, fixing the form and meaning of the prior materials, but... interrogative, exposing the cultural and social conditions of those materials and of the translation or adaptation that has processed them."[23] Venuti argues that this mode of analysis provides a relevant methodology for considering the culture of the adaptor as well as the culture of the adapted text in that:

> *...the application of an interpretant in establishing the new context is never simply interpretive, but potentially interrogative: the formal and thematic differences introduced by the translation or adaptation, the move to a different language and culture or to a different cultural medium with different conditions of production, can invite a critical understanding of the prior materials as well as their originary or subsequent contexts, the linguistic patterns, cultural traditions and social institutions in which they were positioned.*[24]

The idea that White engages in a process of hermeneutical adaptation attuned to both his own culture and the medieval culture of France and England represented by the vernacular literatures will pervade my argument as I consider from which texts, and for what reason, White draws material. Variation in the adaptation of material "is overdetermined by the cultural situation and historical moment in which the adaptation is produced" regardless of whether or not the artist "intends to intervene in political struggles or to take sides in social divisions."[25] Although both translation and adaptation typically claim to be the " 'carrying over' of some irreducible set of features or qualities from one text to another,"[26] this 'carrying over' is inevitably tinged and distorted (as Venuti proposes, almost beyond the artist's conscious decision) by the artist and by the artist's contemporary culture. This is manifest in White's case. Each of the original texts reflects something about its own culture that is lost, or irrelevant, in the culture of its adaptation. However, for an artist such as White, a student of previous cultures laboring to critique both the past and contemporary culture, the semiotics invested in pre-existing works cannot be overlooked. *OFK* can be enjoyed by a reader with no background in medieval studies and his or her interpretation may not be the same as that of a reader who *does* have a background in medieval studies. This is "the context of reception... through which the source text continues to accrue significance when it begins to circulate in its originary culture."[27] In order to discern what White intended to achieve with his adaptation, we must understand that, as John Crane has noted, "White... has felt no compulsion to remain true to anything in the traditional Arthurian legend which did not suit his fancy."[28]

White tailored allusions to, and quotations from, his Arthurian precursors to fit the needs of his narrative and commentary.

The first Lancelot-related example shows the depth of influence embedded in Arthurian texts, simultaneously providing White's view of chivalry in the Middle Ages and in his own time. *IMK* begins with Arthur's voyage to France to recruit the young Lancelot to join his "Order of Chivalry… which goes about fighting against Might."[29] Lancelot explains to Arthur that his Order of Chivalry is called "Fort Mayne in France"[30] and accepts Arthur's offer but explains that he, Lancelot, "must grow up first."[31] As White describes the beginning of Lancelot's training, he directly and indirectly alludes to (at least) five medieval texts, which I will examine in turn. These texts meet up in White's account of Lancelot's dream after Arthur leaves. Lancelot and his brother, Ector Demaris, "got out of [their] chairs and were mounted on two horses. Lancelot said: 'Go we, and seek that which we shall not find.' "[32] In the dream, Lancelot is beaten and despoiled and made to ride an ass instead of a horse, culminating in a scene at a Tantalus-esque well—a portent for the ultimate failure of Camelot and the chivalric Round Table. What concerns us here, however, is Lancelot's line "that which we shall not find." The wording can be found in at least five noteworthy precursor texts. In White's version, Lancelot's dream proclamation occurs as he begins his training as an aspiring knight—what he is seeking in White's version is the pursuit for chivalric perfection. This pursuit will vex Lancelot, and though he will be considered by others to be the best knight, he will remain plagued by self-doubt and self-denial. His quest for that which cannot be found is made explicit later, after he has slept with Elaine, when he laments that "[w]hen I was little… I prayed to God that he would let me work a miracle… I wanted to be the best knight in the world…."[33]

Once the allusions are recognized, Lancelot's pursuit of chivalric perfection can be seen to be analogous to the *Graal*/Grail, which is unattainability made manifest. These allusions are particularly important because they occur when Lancelot is first introduced, thereby establishing his character and ideals. That which cannot be found shifts from adventure (in Wace and *Yvain*), to the unattainable 'Holy Grail' (in the Vulgate Cycle, Post-Vulgate Cycle and Malory), to the unattainable notion of medieval and modern chivalry and courtliness (in White). White almost certainly intended a direct reference to Malory given the other references to Malory throughout— for example, he dedicates the 1938 version of *SS* to "Sir Thomas Maleore, Knight" and concludes *CIW* with Arthur instructing young Tom of Newbold Revel, who is, of course, young Thomas Malory. But it is important to acknowledge and consider Malory's sources with which White might have intended multiple associations.

Tolkien wanted scholars to be satisfied with the ox soup, and not dig around for the bones. Source scholars must always be critical about deciding whether something is a source or not. The instances I will present, which were translated directly from five different but culturally related sources, are too similar to be coincidental. Venuti proposed that the author's culture "overdetermines" the way in which he or she uses source material and, in the same way, the 'original' author's culture overdetermined the production of the source text. My argument examines how White's time and culture were involved in his decisions to allude to specific medieval texts. By considering a brief survey of the scholarship of French and English, which informs the academic culture from which White came, we can see that White's setting was involved in informing his work. White studied at a time during which English and (particularly) French Arthurian literature was advancing as a legitimate field of inquiry. To give a temporal frame of reference, White "matriculated… in [Cambridge] University, on 22 October 1925, having been admitted to Queens' College … He graduated BA on 18 June 1929 and MA, by proxy… on 5 February 1944."[34] Luckily for White, it was only *prior* to "the nineteenth century [that] Old French literature was the domain of gentlemen amateurs."[35] Equally important, around the same time as the canonization of Old French literature "Malory's *Morte* [became] widely accessible in scholarly formats."[36] Slightly before White began at Cambridge, H. Oskar Sommer's seminal seven volume Vulgate Cycle (published in 1909 through 1913) provided scholars with the complete *Lancelot-Graal* Cycle,[37] and aided the understanding of this material by calling it a unified *cycle*. Before Sommer's publication, scholars assumed that these books were non-cyclical. After Sommer, the discovery of the Winchester manuscript of Malory's Arthur in 1934, among other events in medieval scholarship, White had access to materials that had been unavailable to previous medievalists. White's academic culture—Cambridge in the 1920s—bristled with possibility for a young man who wanted to study medieval and Arthurian literature.

Having established the cultural frame from which White worked, I can consider the philological similarities between the five texts from which Lancelot's seeking of "that which cannot be found" resonates. A chronological analysis begins with the twelfth century Norman poet, Wace, and his *Roman de Rou*. Wace writes of the forest Brecheliant[38] "*donc Breton vont sovent fablant*."[39] He describes the fountain of Berenton at which there is "*le perron;/ aler i solent veneor/ a Berenton par grant chalor,/ E a lor cors l'eve espuisier/ E le perron desus moillier;/ por ço soleient pluie aveir;/ Issi soleit jadis ploveir/ En la forest e environ*."[40] This, of course, anticipates Chretien de Troyes' implementation of a magic stone, upon which Calogrenant and Yvain pour water to summon the Otherworld. Jean Frappier identifies this passage from Wace as a source for Chrétien de Troye's *Yvain*. Wace's *Brut* (as well as the *Historia regem brittaniae* of Geoffrey of Monmouth) presents an account "*à la vérité et à la gravité de l'histoire [des] 'merveilles', [des] 'auventures', [des] 'fables' des conteurs bretons (Wace se contente d'y faire une allusion à-demi dédaigneuse)*."[41] Wace acknowledges the Otherworldliness of the forest, by citing the Bretons' claim of fairies inhabiting the woods. The magical qualities of the forest concern my argument less than the narrator's statement that "*La alai jo merveilles querre,/ Vi la forest e vi la terre,/ Merveilles quis, mais nes trovai,/Fol m'en revinc, fol i alai;/ fol i alai, fol m'en revinc,/ Folie quis, por fol me tinc.*"[42] The narrator, here, enters an Otherworldly space, to seek marvels, but finds none.

In Chrétien's *Yvain*, Calogrenant acts as the catalyst for the narrative by recounting his adventures at an Otherworldly spring. Having recently arrived at Arthur's court, Calogrenant narrates his encounter with a hideous peasant, who asks him what he is seeking. In response, Calogrenant identifies himself as "*… uns chevaliers/ Qui quier che que trouver ne puis; Assés ai quis et riens ne truis.*"[43] The adventure that the peasant sends Calogrenant on involves the knight pouring water on a stone, which causes a great storm and summons an Otherworldly knight who defeats Calogrenant in arms and takes his horse. The philological and thematic similarity with Wace is evident. Later in Calogrenant's tale, Chrétien has the knight cite Wace again, saying of his journey into the forest, "*Ensi alai, ensi reving;/ au revenir por fol me ting.*"[44] Lancelot is seeking that which he *shall* not find, and Calogrenant is seeking that which he *cannot* find. What Calogrenant seeks is "*aventures, pour esprouver/ Ma proeche et mon hardement.*"[45] And what Calogrenant finds is that he is a fool for having sought such things.

The link between *Yvain* and the later Vulgate Cycle texts is philologically, if not thematically, evident. Though White would have mostly not been familiar with the Vulgate Cycle, and definitely unaware of the Post-Vulgate Cycle, these crucial texts are intermediaries between Chretien de Troyes and Thomas Malory. Norris Lacy provides the historical context for the Vulgate Cycle, "between 1215 and about 1235, an anonymous author, or group of authors composed the Lancelot-Grail Cycle (also called the Vulgate Cycle, the Prose *Lancelot*, or the Pseudo-Map Cycle)."[46] Within a century, the anonymous authors of the Vulgate Cycle appropriated Calogrenant's experiences into Hector's dream sequence. In this dream, "*lui* [Hector] *et Lancelot del Lac, son frère, descendoient d'une haute chaiere et montoient sor .ii. granz chevax, et disoit li .i. a l'autre: Alons quierre ce que nos ne troverons ja.*"[47] What follows is a description of how Lancelot fell from his horse, was despoiled, and came upon a fountain "*la plus bele qu'il onques viest.*"[48] He tries to drink from it, but the water retreats from him, so he "*retornoit la dom il est venuz.*"[49] In this instance, that which Lancelot (and Hector) will not find is the *Saint Graal.*

In the *Songe d'Helain, d'Hector, et de Gaivain* from the Post-Vulgate Cycle, Arthur is the central figure, as opposed to the Lancelot and Guinevere focus of the Vulgate Cycle.[50] Difficulty arises in working with the Post-Vulgate Cycle in a philological way because "some portions of the Post-Vulgate have been lost; others are known only in fragmentary form or through early translations into Spanish or Portuguese."[51] It is Bogdanow's reconstruction from which I draw:

> *Esta visam vio Galvam, mas Estor vio outra mui maravilhosa e dessemelhada desta, ca lhe semelhava que elle e seu iraão La[n]çaroc deciam de huã cadeira e sobiam sobre dous cavallos grandes, e diziam huã ao outro:*
>
> *—Vaamos buscar o que nom poderemos achar ja.*
>
> *E asi adarom per muitas jornadas, tanto, atee que Lançaroc caya do cavallo e derribava- o huã homem, que depois fazia sobir em huã asno, e espia-o da rroupa e de quanto lhe achava. E depois sobia no asno e andava asi longo tempo, ataa que chegava a huã fonte, a mais fremossa nem a mais saborossa que nunca vira, e decia hi por bever, e hu queria bever, f<u>gia-lhe [a] agoa. E quando vi[a] que lhe fugia, tornava-sse pera donde viera.*[52]

Thus, we can rightly assume that this line "Let's go seek what we can't find" resonated from the Old French to the Portuguese translators. In addition, in both the Old French Post-Vulgate and the Portuguese (re)iteration, we see the same scenario wherein Lancelot falls from his horse and is made to ride a donkey. The symbolism of the *chevalier* who is deprived of his *cheval* and made to ride the inferior *âne* should not go unnoticed.

Related semiotic extensions of the key line—associating it with the grail, of the ass, and of the spring—carry over from the French Vulgate and Post Vulgate Cycles to Malory's work. Though Malory's representation of this passage is translated from French to English, he uses the same Grail-context from the Vulgate Cycle and the same narrative framework for the line spoken by the two knights. In Ector's vision, "hit semed hym that hys brothir, sir Launcelot, and he alyghte oute of a chayre and lepte upon two horsis. And the one s[a]yde to the other, 'Go we to seke that we shall nat fynde.' And hym thought thatt a man bete sir Launcelot and dispoyled... and sette hym upon an asse."[53]

To a reader unfamiliar with medieval literature, Lancelot's derivative declaration in *OFK* would seem like a casual observation about the trials of chivalry, with no especial significance. However to a medievalist aware of the intertexts involved in this case, the textual and historical resonances of the line must complicate a literary interpretation of White's version of Lancelot and his quest. The use of the borrowed line can be read in three registers. First, the statement is, frankly, opaque—Lancelot is seeking that which cannot be found. He is a knight. Knights go on quests, but how the quest might end seems not to be at stake. The second register depends on our recognition that this line is lifted from a medieval text telling the story of a very different knight. The intertextuality in this case gives Lancelot a sort of medieval wrapping, making him seem as if he is a more authentic representation of chivalry because he speaks with the voice of an historical representation of knighthood. As I will show later, Lancelot's genuinely *medieval* nature is doubtful, or at least more complicated. The third register relates to the other two, in that recognition of precursor texts leads us to understand the incongruity of these texts and, therefore, the strange artifice, even emptiness, of Lancelot. The way in which White uses precursor texts (occasionally mentioning the source, occasionally directly appropriating without mentioning the source) resembles the way in which medieval authors used their source materials (such as Malory's own use of the "Freynshhe Booke."[54] While the use of this technique alludes to an authentically medieval narrative and seems to grant medieval verisimilitude to Lancelot, in fact, this use initiates the critique of the *Graal*-like unattainability of medieval and modern chivalry that White will pursue throughout the tetralogy. Combined with White's use of the analogy of chivalry as a Holy Grail-like entity—that which cannot be found—White's commentary on chivalry becomes clear. I submit that this emptiness of Lancelot functions metonymically as White's critique of the foundations of chivalry as a whole. In the end, it does not matter if White had direct knowledge of these texts; he certainly would have had no knowledge of the yet-undiscovered French or Portuguese version of the Post-Vulgate Cycle. But White tapped into this pedigree of resonance, and allowed it to inform his iteration of Arthurian legend, and that is significant.

The later depictions of Lancelot's medieval nature provides another set of keys to understanding White's overarching criticism of chivalry. The first instance was the allusion to the medieval material that I have unpacked. Following these examples is White's depiction of Lancelot's medieval nature. On several occasions, White directly labels Lancelot as "medieval." In Chapter Six of *IMK*, White describes that Lancelot is more than "an ugly young man who was good at games", in fact, "he was a knight with a medieval respect for honor."[55] Lancelot considered this medieval respect for honor, "to have a Word", "to be the most valuable of possessions."[56] Later, White begins to reveal that Lancelot's medievalness might not be entirely valid. Lancelot continues to lament his lost virginity:

> *for he put a higher value on chastity than is fashionable in our century. He believed, like the man in Lord Tennyson, that people could only have the strength of ten on account of their hearts being pure. It so happened that his strength was as the strength of ten, and such was the medieval explanation which had been discovered for it.*[57]

Here, White does not use the adjective "medieval" to directly describe Lancelot—though it describes the explanation for his strength; however, this line does point even the casual reader towards the blending of Tennyson's Victorian chivalry and the chivalry of Malory (and his sources). To a casual reader, White develops Lancelot as a "medieval" knight through his various descriptions, but on closer inspection, we can see that White is critical of medieval chivalric culture in a way that may have anticipated modern notions of chivalry. White's third and fourth books deal extensively with Lancelot and his relationship with Guinevere. At a time when Lancelot felt his "sentiment for Guinevere was an ignoble sentiment," White explains that "to a medieval nature like Lancelot's, with its fatal weakness for loving the highest when he saw it, this was a position of pain."[58] Here, White is claiming explicit medievalness for Lancelot. And yet, this declaration of Lancelot's "medieval nature" is not as simple as that, *because its source isn't medieval.*

The precursor text from which White draws this line is Lord Alfred Tennyson's *Idylls of the King*. White mentioned Tennyson's treatment of Guinevere, as opposed to Malory's less kind treatment of her, in a letter to Potts from October of 1939,[59] establishing that White was familiar with Tennyson's *Idylls*. In the poem-chapter *Guinevere*, the eponymous queen provides an exegesis for her relationship with Lancelot, and her regret that she "could not breathe in that fine air, | That pure severity of perfect light— | [she] yearn'd for warmth and color which [she] found | In Lancelot."[60] She explains that she felt unworthy to be in the company of King Arthur, whom she then extols as "the highest and most human, too, | Not Lancelot, nor another."[61] Her soliloquy ends with lines from which White must have surely drawn:

> *What might I not have made of thy fair world,*
> *Had I but loved thy highest creature here?*
> *It was my duty to have loved the highest;*
> *We needs must love the highest when we see it,*
> *Not Lancelot, nor another.*[62]

Again, as was the case with his chivalric quest, Lancelot's words, at a key point in establishing his character, are lifted from a precursor text. In this case, an element of White's claim that Lancelot has a medieval nature comes from a nineteenth-century text in which Guinevere explains that Lancelot is not the highest knight, but rather, it is Arthur whom she must love. The intertexts multiply and chain together here: White sets up a wrapping of medievalness that can be taken at face value, but then undermines this declaration by using an incongruous precursor text, which we may again assume would have been familiar to someone steeped in the medieval literature and its modern revisions.

To the casual reader, Sir Lancelot du Lac certainly seems a medieval figure. He seeks that which cannot be found; he is the best knight on unattainable chivalric quest. But his quest is ultimately hollow and incomplete—he does not succeed in attaining the Grail and his chivalric successes amount to aiding the destruction of Camelot. Malory also contains this critique of chivalry—the best knight loves the queen and the kingdom falls. Malory also pulls from precursor texts. The difference between Malory's and White's use of precursor texts that White wrote in a time where the incorporation of precursor texts is of particular significance in contrast to a medieval method of literary production, where such incorporation was the norm. White describes Lancelot's nature as 'medieval' but he informs the knight with modern paradoxes and ironies of intertexuality which are not medieval because—ironically—they are transhistorical parodies of medieval method. And that is the comment that White is making on modern and medieval chivalry: it is that which cannot be found. The ideal of chivalry rarely reflected true medieval knighthood—Malory understood this to some extent—and the fatality of this misunderstood chivalry manifests in England before and during World War II.

In addition to complicating Lancelot's character, the appearance of Tennyson's line indicates White's criticism of the socio-cultural idea of "duty" in England before and during World War II. If White's line is juxtaposed with Tennyson's then White is saying that chivalric "duty" is "fatal weakness." Guinevere speaks of loving the highest as a duty; Lancelot speaks of loving the highest as a fatal weakness and a position of pain. Therefore, given White's self-expressed disdain for war, yet occasional guilt for not aiding the English war effort, he adds yet another critique of the individual's duty to authority. The fatal duty facing the young "knights" of England in the early 20th century was that of World War II and, before that, World War I. Lancelot's fatal duty contributed to the collapse of the utopian Camelot. Through both obvious and veiled episodes in *OFK*, White touts his anti-war stance and his lament for the utopian potential of Europe in the nineteenth century ruined by the World Wars.

The final book of *OFK* depicts Arthur requesting a young page, Tom of Newbold Revell near Warrick (Thomas Malory), to abstain from the upcoming battle with Mordred "to tell everybody that would listen about this ancient idea [chivalry], which both of them had once thought good," but which in the end had failed.[63] During the period in which White was writing this book, World War II had loomed and then broken out in Europe. The chivalric themes of Might and Right with which Arthur grapples throughout the tetralogy are, unmistakably and anachronistically, relevant to this historical context. The final words of the book reference a tenet of Arthurian legend that the king will return to England in times of crisis: "*explicit liber regis quondam regisque futuri.*"[64] Using Arthurian legend, White proposes the answer not only to the impossibly ideal medieval chivalric code, but also to the political crises of modern Europe—and here's where the geese of Arthur's *Sword in the Stone*-youth come back in:

> *There would be a day—there must be a day—when he [Arthur] would come back to Gramarye with a new Round Table which had no corners, just as the world had none—a table without boundaries between the nations who would sit to feast there. The hope of making it would lie in culture. If people could be persuaded to read and write, not just to eat and make love, there was still a chance that they might come to reason.*[65]

White continues this rationale in a 1940 letter to Potts, in which he proposes, "the central theme of Morte d'Arthur [*sic*] is to find an antidote to war."[66] The time during which Malory wrote was a similarly tumultuous period for the English people. The Hundred Years' War (1337–1453), between France and England, had just concluded and England was entering a time of internal strife known as the War of the Roses (1455–1485). The English people looked to stories, such as those of Arthur, for nationalistic reassurance. If a story is important enough to be passed down, it resonates with a national (or international) audience and the Arthuriad is one of those stories. Arthur's conceived utopia could not endure and it seemed that Europe was falling to forces of Might over Right. White offers a critique of Might, even Might for Right, at a time when Might and Might for Right were being called into question in England and on an unprecedented global scale. In order to provide a comfort to the English people, "Malory's immediate purpose was to create a type of the ideal knight and the foremost among all of

Arthur's knights. His larger purpose was to show Lancelot and the court to which he belonged in a prelapsarian state, preceding and tragically contrasting with the corruption and downfall to come."[67] Whether it was Arthur's sin of incest and Mordred or Lancelot and Guinevere's transgression, ultimately, it was Might, despite Arthur's attempt to use Might for Right, which destroyed Camelot. Like Camelot, Europe in the 19th century appeared to have had a utopian potential; however, Might destroyed both of these potentials. Gallix describes White's time in Ireland as vexing for him because he "could never quite reconcile himself with the idea that he was taking no active part in the war activities."[68] White eventually came to view the writing of *OFK* as "an antidote to war" and as his contribution to the war effort. He resurrected Arthur to give hope to the English people in their time of need, just as Arthur himself was promised to do. White joins the company of Lewis, Tolkien and Malory in offering the English people a myth of national self-invention and self–reliance—steeped in lore and nostalgia, but culturally reflective of the contemporary period. And, as important, a myth whose relations to its sources were deeply troubled.

Endnotes

1. This article represents the incipient stages of a much longer project, which will culminate in an annotated version of, or companion to, *The Once and Future King*. I believe that there is sufficient precursor material and that that material is significant enough to warrant a revisited, annotated edition that will highlight White's allusions to and adaptations of precursor material, which were often quite significant to the understanding of 20th century socio-political tensions, such as WWII and Anglo-Irish tensions, as well as an understanding of the evolution of medieval studies as a field, medievalism and medieval literature itself.
2. Henceforth I will refer to the following titles by the bracketed abbreviations: *The Once and Future King* [OFK], *The Sword in the Stone* [SS], *The Queen of Air and Darkness* [QAD], *The Witch in the Wood* [WW], *The Ill-Made Knight* [IMK], and *The Candle in the Wind* [CIW].
3. I will primarily consider the text of 1958 compilation, *OFK*. When I refer to the individual books, it will be assumed that I am referring to the versions within *OFK*, unless otherwise noted. I will account for textual variations if there are significant differences. Though White considered *The Book of Merlyn* to be part of his series, I will not discuss it, though I will remain cognizant of it—especially in lieu of White's changing relationship to Malory and his increased understanding and rejection of war. Though I refer to *OFK* as a tetralogy, I am aware that White technically meant for his series to be a pentalogy.
4. T. H. White and François Gallix, *Letters to a Friend: The Correspondence between T. H. White and L. J. Potts* (New York: Putnam, 1982).
5. Heather Worthington, "From Children's Story to Adult Fiction: T. H. White's *The Once and Future King*" in *Arthuriana*. 12.2 (Summer 2002), 98.
6. *Ibid.* 106
7. Elisabeth Brewer notes that "White possessed several copies of Malory, [but] he seems to have worked from the Globe edition edited by Sir Edward Strachey, which he heavily annotated.... The Globe edition prints Caxton's version of 1485...." Brewer catalogs, in addition to his Globe Edition, that White also had "the Dent Everyman edition of Caxton (1935); *Arthur Pendragon*, New York, George Putnam's Sons, 1943; and Vinaver's first edition of the Winchester MS, *The Works of Thomas Malory*, Oxford 1947." See Elisabeth Brewer, *T.H. White's the Once and Future King* (Cambridge, England: D. S. Brewer, 1993), 211.
8. Jason Fisher, *Tolkien and the Study of His Sources: Critical Essays* (Jefferson, N.C: McFarland & Co, 2011), 2.

9. Ibid., 1
10. Ibid., 30
11. C. S. Lewis and Walter Hooper, *Studies in Medieval and Renaissance Literature* (Cambridge: Cambridge University Press, 1966), 36.
12. Fisher, 33
13. I do not wish to enter the fray over Tolkien and source criticism. I am not making a claim about Tolkien; rather, I am putting into practice the theory of source criticism that focuses on Tolkien because it closely resembles the work that I must to do with White.
14. E. L. Risden, "Tolkien and source criticism: remarking and remaking," in Jason Fisher, ed., *Tolkien and the Study of His Sources: Critical Essays* (Jefferson, N.C: McFarland & Co, 2011), 14–16.
15. Ibid., 21
16. In a previous project, I have traced the mutations of the character Mordred from the first mention of him to the works of Malory. In doing so, I noticed that almost none of the cycles were static—even the most famous, such as the Grail Cycle and the Guinevere-Lancelot Cycle.
17. The versions of Arthurian legend that manifest after the Vulgate Cycle contain most of the elements more commonly associated with the modern conception of the legend: Lancelot as Guinevere's lover, the Grail Cycle, the incestuous birth of Mordred.
18. *BOM*, xi
19. Brewer, 82–83
20. Risden, 21, 22
21. Ibid., 20
22. Lawrence Venuti, "Adaptation, Translation, Critique." *Journal of Visual Culture* 6.1 (2007): 25–43. Available from http://vcu.sagepub.com/content/6/1/25.full.pdf, accessed April 5, 2014.
23. Ibid., 41
24. Ibid., 38
25. Ibid., 27. We must remember that though Venuti considers filmic adaptation of literatures in his article, here, his general theory of adaptation remains relevant to White's tetralogy. Film directors adapting literature are very similar to medieval authors adapting the literatures of their predecessors. Both artists are expected to produce more or less faithful adaptations of prior material, and to adapt that material to the specific medial contexts and constraints of the new work; this is not considered plagiarism or intellectual theft. In fact, in some cases, the more faithfully reproduced the adaptation is, the more critical praise it receives. For a medieval example of this, consider the work of monastic scribes who were tasked with creating replicas of illuminated manuscripts; this was not considered a mindless task of copying (in the modern sense) but rather a high artistic endeavor.
26. Ibid., 29
27. Ibid., 29
28. John Crane, *T. H. White* (New York: Twayne Publishers, 1974), 77.
29. *IMK*, 316.
30. White enters the nineteenth century tradition of *le mal anglais* with the mismatched gender, *la main* being feminine, and the adjective *fort* referring to a masculine. Additionally, the multiple Old French definitions of *main* ("hand, human body, power, authority, safeguard, condition, people, dwelling, and lodging" [Calin, email]) complicate the meaning of this phrase. Regardless of the exact translation, Lancelot refers to the French version of Arthur's contemplation of Might and Right.
31. *IMK*, 316
32. Ibid., 317
33. Ibid., 376
34. Jacqueline Cox citing UA Graduati 12/251, email correspondence with the author, July 4, 2012.
35. Keith Busby and Jane H. M. Taylor. "French Arthurian Literature" in Norris Lacy, ed., *A History of Arthurian Scholarship* (Cambridge: D.S. Brewer, 2006), 96.

36. Roger Dalrymple, "English Arthurian Literature" in Lacy, 142.
37. Busby and Taylor, 96
38. The modern spelling is Brocéliande, which is the modern day Breton forest of Paimpont.
39. All translations henceforth are my own, unless otherwise noted: "of which Breton have often told tales." Robert Wace and A J. Holden, *Le roman de Rou de Wace* (Paris: A. & J. Picard, 1970), line 6374.
40. Ibid., 6378–6384: "a quarried stone;/ and there in the past, hunters/ at Berenton [the fountain] from a great heat/ would draw up water in their hunting horns,/ and moisten the top of the stone/ because of this, it used to rain/ for this, often in the past, it rained/ in the forest and the [surrounding] region."
41. "...of the truth, of the seriousness of the account [of] the 'marvels', the 'adventures', the 'fables' of the Breton story tellers (to which Wace contents himself with making a semi-contemptuous allusion [to the Breton storytellers])." Jean Frappier, *Le Roman Breton, Yvain: Ou, Le Chevalier Au Lion* (Paris: Centre de Documentation Universitaire, 1958), 38.
42. Wace and Holden, 6392–6399. "I went here to see marvels [marvelous things]/ I saw the forest, and I saw the country,/ Marvels I sought, but I did not find./ Foolish, I returned, foolish, I went./Foolish I went [and] foolish I returned/ I sought foolishness [foolish things], consequently, I recognize I was fool."
43. "...a knight, who seeks that which I cannot find; enough have I sought, and I find nothing." Chrétien de Troyes and Jean-Marie Fritz, *Romans: suivis de chansons; Avec, En Appendice, Philomena* (Paris: Librairie générale française, 2005), lines 365–6.
44. "Thus I went, thus I returned;/ Upon returning, I consider myself a fool." Chrétien de Troyes and William W. Kibler, *The Knight with the Lion,Or, Yvain* (New York, N.Y: Garland, 1985), lines 78–9.
45. "adventures, to prove [his] bravery and [his] strength." De Troyes and Fritz, 360–1.
46. Norris J. Lacy, *Lancelot-Grail: the Old French Arthurian Vulgate and post-Vulgate in translation.* (New York: Garland Publishing, 1992), xi.
47. Fanni Bogdanow and Anne Berrie. *La quête du saint-graal: roman en prose du xiiie siècle* (Paris: Librairie générale française, 2006), 386–8. "he and Lancelot du Lac, his brother, descended from a high chair and mounted on two big horses, and said to each other, one to the other: Let's go to seek that which we will not find."
48. Ibid. Trans.: "...the most beautiful [fountain] that he had ever seen."
49. Ibid. Trans.: "... returns [to] the place [from which] he came."
50. Lacy, xi
51. Ibid., xi
52. Bogdanow, 205–6. "This vision Gawain saw, but Hector saw another, marvelous and different from Gawaine's, for it seemed to him that he and his brother Lancelot came down off a single chair and got on two large horses. They said to each other, "Let's go seek what we won't be able to find." Thus they rode many days, until Lancelot fell off his horse and a man knocked him down, then made him get on a donkey, stripping him of his clothes and everything he had. After he had got on the donkey, he rode for a long time, until he arrived at a spring, the most beautiful and desirable he had ever seen. He dismounted to drink from it, but when he tried to drink, the water receded from him. When he saw that it receded from him, he returned to where he had come from." Trans. Marsha Asher, quoted in Lacy, 155.
53. Thomas Malory and Eugène Vinaver, *Works [of] Malory* (Oxford: Oxford University Press, 1977), 559.
54. Ibid., 676
55. *IMK,* 338
56. Ibid., 339
57. Ibid., 368
58. Ibid., 387

59. Sylvia Warner, *T. H. White; a Biography* (New York: Viking Press, 1968), 150.
60. Alfred, Lord Tennyson, *Idylls of the King, and a Selection of Poems* (New York: New American Library, 1961), 239–40.
61. Ibid., 240
62. Ibid., 240
63. *OFK*, 636
64. "Here ends the book of the once and future king." Ibid., 639.
65. Ibid., 639
66. Warner, 178
67. Albert Hartung, "Narrative Technique, Characterization, and the Sources in Malory's "Tale of Sir Lancelot" in *Studies in Philology*, vol. 70 no. 3 (July, 1973): 252.
68. Gallix, 93

FRANCHISE AND CHIVALRIC IDENTITY

Michael A. Cramer

In the jargon of performance studies, performance refers to truth, to the highlighting and playing the essence of a thing, and theatricality to falsehood, to the disguises and trappings, costumes, sets and pretend emotions that make theatre theater. The theatricality of the Middle Ages, particularly the culture of chivalry, has long been commented on. Knighthood required certain props, costume, and attitudes. It had conventions and very formal conduct. But, in the nature of performance, it was supposed to be done well enough that it became not a sham but an expression of the essence of the actor. This is where I wish to start when looking at the chivalric virute known as "franchise." In *Chivalry,* Keen defined Franchise as "the free and frank bearing that gives visible testimony to the combination of good birth with virtue."[1] When examined closely, this definition is very performative. Knighthood is a role to be played, and a good knight is supposed to play it well. If indeed franchise is a virtue, then it has as much to do with performance, with the essence of a thing, as with the theatrical. But among reenactors, Franchise is often described in theatrical terms. To many, it simply means "looking the part." If this were true, however, anybody in a coat of mail could call himself a knight—which is, of course, exactly what they are doing: but do they truly have "franchise" if what they do is merely dress up and pretend to be knights? This paper will attempt to answer that question by examining different ideas about franchise.

Franchise is very hard to nail down. It is a virtue that doesn't quite fit. French dictionaries often define "franchise" as *sincérité* and occasionally give the English translation as "frankness." One dictionary of Old French defines it as "privilege." A more common word in French chivalry, which appears in numerous early knighting ceremonies is *preux,* as part of the knights basic oath *sois preux. Preux* is normally translated as "valiant" or "courageous", and has little use in modern French outside its connection with chivalry. *Preux* is also synonymous with the noun "worthy," as in one who is worthy of praise. Eustache Deschamps referred to the Nine Worthies (the nine models of chivalry that every knight should follow: Hector, Ceasar, Alexander, Joshua, David, Judas Macabeas, Charlegmane, Arthur, and Geofrey de Boulion) as the *neuf preux.*[2] Carl Stephenson says, "Of the many formulas that might be spoken while delivering the accolade, the most eloquent was also the briefest: *Sois preux!* To be *preux* was to conduct oneself as a true knight; nothing more."[3] But this same description is often given to franchise. Stephanson goes on to say that to act in a knightly manner the knight should follow examples, most notably Roland, who displayed prowess, piety, valor, and above all loyalty to his lord (Stephanson does not mention the word "franchise," but its commonly understood meaning was there in his definition of *preux*). This is what Huizinga was speaking of when he said, "The life of a knight was an imitation."[4]

The normal virtues—charity, humility, chastity, etc.—tell us how we should act. We should be humble, give to the poor, and resist the temptations of the flesh. Franchise, if it is to be considered a virtue, must also tell us how to act. It cannot be simply how we dress, can it? This seems to be how many modern re-creationists look at it. In discussing franchise with Society for Creative Anachronism (SCA) knights or reenactors, they often define "franchise" as simply looking the part, of wearing armor and clothing appropriate to a gentleman warrior of the middle ages. How one looks is all important in this version of Franchise, and the guys with the most beautiful armor are said to have it. In *Medieval Fantasy as Performance,* I rather pithily wrote "clothes make the knight." I was stating the obvious fact that when we are recreating the middle ages it is our clothes that code us as medieval, augmented by the props we use in our performances of medievalism. In other words, what makes us medieval is theatrical. We are still modern people with modern bodies living in a modern world pretending to be knights and damsels and we are still to a great extent bound by modern conventions. As I said at the time, if an SCA knight behaved as was proper for a medieval knight, they would cart him off to jail: but if franchise means behaving as a knight then that calls my statement about clothes and knighthood into question.

Some re-enactors, following Keen, define it as an attitude of liberality and honesty, a determined innocence. Not all of them are agreed, however, that it is a virtue. Some of them can make no sense of it at all. Some people can see clearly why charity, courage, and humility are virtues, because they dictate behavior. Franchise dictates nothing save an attitude or, worse yet, a certain sartorial extravagance. James Cromwell, a chivalric re-enactor who runs a private, professional "school of knighthood" in Chico California, considers franchise to be a false virtue, one that simply cannot be justified as such.[5]

Scholar and re-enactor Brian Price lists the Chivalric virtues as Prowess, Justice, Loyalty, Defense, Courage, Faith, Humility, Largesse, Nobility, and, last, Franchise. Of Franchise he says, "Seek to emulate everything I have spoken of as sincerely as possible, not for the reason of personal gain but because it is right. Do not restrict your exploration to a small world, but seek to infuse every aspect of your life with these qualities. Should you succeed in even a tiny measure then you will be well remembered for your quality and virtue."[6] He doesn't source this list, saying only that it is based on "an old code." It is significant here that he lists nobility as a separate virtue, since "holding to the virtues of a knight" as he puts it is what many medieval people would have defined as franchise, as we shall see.

Dana Kramer-Rolls takes a different view of franchise. It is not and never was a virtue. It is the power vested in a knight when he receives the accolade. To have "franchise" is to have the power and the authority to act as a knight. "I always took Franchise as the right and license given to you by the King to do in his name—correct wrongs, wage wars etc.... as in a Franchise via the economic view where you get the rights of the larger system to uphold certain standards and forms."[7]

Modern scholars have no idea how to treat franchise as a virtue. There is no modern frame of reference for it. For instance, In *Sir Gwaine and the Green Knight, fraunchyse* is one of the five virtues listed in the famous five-times-five section, which describes the meaning of the pentangle on Gawain's shield: " þe fyft fyue þat I finde þat þe frek vsed | Watz fraunchyse and felawschyp forbe al þyng."[8] Modern translations don't know what to do with this. Jamie Weston, back in 1898, translated the passage as "And the fifth five that the hero used were frankness and fellowship above all..."[9] In 1999, W.A. Nielson translated it as "The fifth five that I find that the hero used were generosity and fellowship above all things..."[10]

In the anonymous *Arthur and Gwain,* Gwain brings several men before Arthur and says of one of them:

> *And this other gentilman that is of so grete bewté, that is so moche and semly and well shapen of body and of alle membres, is nevew to the emperour of Costantynnoble, and his name is Seigramor; and [he] is come with us be his debonerté and his fraunchise to take armes, and that ye hym make knyght. (95–98)*[11]

The footnote to this edition defines "moche" as "large," "semly" as "handsome" and "debonerté" as "courtesy" (though in an early note it is "virtue"), but doesn't see a need to define "fraunchise." The editor either thought the reader would understand or had no clue himself what it meant.

In "The Siege of Thebes," Lydgate writes that when death comes for a man:

> *Than geyneth nat to his savacioun*
> *Neyther fraunchyse nor proteccioun,*
> *And lit or noght may helpen in this caas*
> *Sauffecondit or supersedyas. (3429–3432)*[12]

A margin note defines it as "freedom from arrest" and an accompanying footnote, citing the MED, says the term "refers broadly to freedom and nobility of character and specifically to special rights and privileges, including right of sanctuary and freedom from arrest in certain places. The MED itself defines *fraunchise* as:

> *1. (a) Freedom (as opposed to servitude), the social status of a freeman (whether by birth or by manumission); (b) national sovereignty, independence; (c) spiritual freedom; esp., the privileged state of Adam and Eve before the fall; (d) freedom of action (without social or political implications), freedom to do as one pleases.*
>
> *2. (a) Nobility of character, magnanimity; liberality, generosity; a noble or generous act; (b) lofty manner; (c) of gold: a noble quality, a virtue.*[13]

The dictionary then lists four other definitions having to do with privilege. This supports both ideas about franchise, franchise not as a virtue but as an authority granted by the accolade, and franchise as nobility of character. Likewise, the Anglo-Norman Dictionary lists as definitions:

> *1. free status (as opposed to serfdom or villeinage); (law) liberation, making free of a serf or villein*
>
> *2. freedom (of will), free will; (law) (state of) freedom, liberty; (law) a special right, privilege or exemption, granted to an individual, corporate body, etc.; (law) a corporate body, such as a town or gild, enjoying special privileges; (law) citizenship, membership of a corporate body, such as a town or gild, enjoying special privileges; (law) an area of land, such as a seignory or a borough, over which special privileges are operative; (fig.) privileged area; (law) a court belonging to a franchise*
>
> *3. nobility (of character), distinction, excellence; considerateness, kindness, generosity.*

It is only in the second definition from the MED, and the third definition from the Anglo-Norman dictionary, that we see any semblance of the franchise that Keen writes about: but in both these cases the word is being used as an adjective and not a noun. There is nothing here of franchise as a virtue (freedom from arrest certainly seems to be what Lydgate is discussing).

Looking for the virtue of franchise in literature is dicey. In the "Knight of the Cart," for instance, Kay refuses to get into the dwarf's cart because it is beneath his dignity as a knight. Lancelot does so because to him rescuing Guinevere is more important than his own pride. Indeed, it can be seen as an act of humility, another knightly virtue, for Lancelot to consent to be so degraded. When we consider the story in terms of franchise as opposed to humility, the action becomes murkier. If franchise is indeed acting and appearing in all ways as a knight would appear and act, then what Lancelot did was a sin. He was not being virtuous in getting into the knight's cart, stressing his own humility. The knight is supposed to be humble before God, but in the presence of peasants to humble oneself goes against the hierarchical order which, to the medieval knight, God has imposed upon the world. It is inappropriate for a knight to be seen in the presence of the people except through the mediation of the horse.[14] A knight who is not on horseback, when among the people, is not a knight. The horse elevates the knight both physically and socially—certainly economically. But the cart is a vehicle for work. Its sole purpose is to be employed in labor. It is a conveyance of the laboring class, and in this case, as a death cart, it has a darker symbolism. It is sinful for Lancelot to get into the cart, and Kay knows this. Lancelot commits a class sin by getting into the cart. He commits a sin against franchise.

When we consider Ramon Lull and what he had to say about knightly virtues, we don't find franchise mentioned. In *The Book of Knighthood and Chivalry*, Lull differentiates between knightly attributes and virtues. Book Eight is devoted entirely to those virtues that a knight should follow, but he lists the standard seven: Faith, Hope, Charity, Justice, Prudence, Strength, and Temperance.[15] Franchise does not get a mention. Book Three, on the other hand, is dedicated to the "Office that a knight should maintain" (as Caxton translated it), and here Lull lists off several things that pertain to what most people view as franchise, both franchise as authority and franchise as bearing. A knight should protect women, defend the church, govern lands and dispense both justice and mercy. He should partake in sport. He must defend his lord. He must be witty and discrete. He must have the wealth to support his office. He must police the land. He must not be a robber. And, of course, he must have a good horse.[16] Though he doesn't use the term, Book Three of Lull is the best primer on franchise written.

Like the other virtues, franchise is not strictly a knightly virtue. It is just as often ascribed to women, who don't in most romances take the accolade. In "The Merchant's Tale," Chaucer writes of the young wife May, "Lo, pity runneth soon in gentle heart! Heere may ye see how excellent franchise | In wommen is, whan they hem narwe avyse," which in the modern English is rendered "Here may you see what generosity | In women is when they advise closely."[17] Generosity is a far cry from frankness, but perhaps not from liberality. Chaucer, of course, is being facetious. May's generosity is toward the young man Daimian, who has begged her to be his lover and to cuckold her old husband January. Such generosity is virtuous only in Chaucer's sarcastic world.

A clear use of franchise as a virtue can be found in John Gowers' *Cinkante Balades* (Fifty Ballads). In ballad XXVIII, a knight pleads for a favor from his lady, saying:

Les vertus de franchise et de largesce
Jeo sai, ma dame, en vous sont establi;
Et vous savetz ma peine et ma destresce,
Dont par dolour jeo sui sempres faili
En le defalte soul de vo merci,
Q'il ne vous plest un mot a moi mander:
Om voit sovent de petit poi doner.

The translation reads:

The virtues of liberality and largesse
I know, my lady, are established in you;
And you know my pain and my distress.
Thus I am always falling into sadness
In the lack alone of your mercy,
That it does not please you to send a word to me.
Often one sees little being given.[18]

Here franchise is translated as "liberality." The knight wishes her to be liberal with her favors. It is the same sense franchise, far from virtuous, that Chaucer spoke of: franchise is being free with her sexual favors. But surely "frankness," while it would change the meaning, might work as well. If indeed franchise refers to the free and frank bearing expected of a knight, might it not also be the free and frank bearing expected of a lady? In that case the knight would be pleading with the lady to freely and frankly give her heart to him (In ballad L, Gower also uses franchise as the virtue of a lady).

Consider for a moment the possibility that franchise is an expression of the essence of a thing. The essence of knighthood is a free and frank masculinity, a testosterone-fueled longing for violence that is only checked by service to his liege, to God, or to a lady. All of chivalric literature turns at some point on the need to control the knight, to direct his violent tendencies toward lofty goals. This was the agenda behind both crusades and courtly love. What then is woman's essence? The controlling factors are reputation, duty to God and husband, and the virtue of chastity. But in all of medieval romantic literature, women are highly sexualized. Their purpose on earth, within the medieval patriarchy certainly, is procreation, therefore their essence is sex. Women are to be worshiped, to be adored, but it is always for the desire of sexual favors. The game of courtly love is a teasing game, as Gawain experiences all too clearly. The woman is never supposed to relent. May, of course, does, as did many a wife relent to the advances of a young squire, but relenting to both Lydgate and Chaucer was an expression of the woman's franchise. Virtuous in the traditional sense it is not, but in more earthly sense it is. If franchise is the free and frank expression of a one's essence, then in the knight this would be a self-assured masculinity and in the woman a free and frank sexuality. Seen in this way, franchise *is* performance.

There is really no way to translate Franchise in to modern English. As a signifier, the concept toward which the word points no longer exists in the modern mind. Both versions of franchise are correct. Franchise is, indeed, nobility of bearing and of character, the free and frank masculinity of a privileged warrior class. It means quite simply to act as a knight should act. However, one can only act as a knight if one *is* a knight. You can't just buy a plot of land, sit a horse, and call yourself a knight. Franchise involves more than that. You must have the accolade. In return for your service you are given the state and office of "knight," with privileges and authority as well as obligations and duties. The knight served his lord and in return was granted an income, often land, and with it the duty to maintain his office and the right to dispense justice and to play the knight. Maintaining that office was not merely a matter of bureaucracy. It was not simply a matter of policing the land in times of peace and defending it in times of war. It was also performative. It meant dressing the part, keeping a court, doing those things which a knight ought to do. A knight was not a knight without the accolade, without service to his lord, but he was also not a knight without the wit, discretion, horse, and good acts that were expected of him. This is the performance of knighthood. This is franchise.

Re-enactors and scholars would be wise to take note: knighthood is, indeed, a performance. Lull's ideal of knighthood involved not only the actions of the knight but the props and costumes as well—the horse, the armor, even the clothes. Gawain and Sagamore were knights not just because of the accolade but also because of the way they carried themselves. The Middle Ages were indeed a theatrical time, and a knight was one of the main performers on this stage. Franchise is only a virtue if knighthood is performative. In the romantic tradition, a knight has an obligation to maintain the dignity of knighthood, to cut a noble figure, to quite literally act like a knight.

Chivalry is a performance. It is the buckling of the spurs and the girding on of the sword, it is donning the armor and taking the field, it is doing all of those things that Castiglione lists as being necessary for a courtier and that Lull lists as maintaining the office of knighthood. It is a performance with conventions, costume, motivations, even on occasion a script. In this milieu acting the part of a knight, having that free and frank bearing, looking the part, is indeed a virtue.

Endnotes

1. Maurice Keen, *Chivalry* (New Haven: Yale University Press, 1984), 2.
2. Johan Huizinga, *The Waning of the Middle Ages* (New York: St. Martins Press, 1924), 61.
3. Carl Stephenson, *Medieval Feudalism* (Ithaca, NY: Cornell University Press, 1942), 50.
4. Huizinga, 60
5. James Cromwell, private correspondence with the author.
6. Brian Price, "A Code of Chivalry" (1997), available from http://www.gonderzone.org/Library/Chivalry/code.htm, accessed May 7, 2012.
7. Dana Kramer-Rolls, private correspondence with the author.
8. *Sir Gawain and the Green Knight,* ed. J.R.R. Tolkien and E.V. Gordon (Oxford: Clarendon Press, 1967). Available from http://quod.lib.umich.edu/cgi/t/text/text-idx?c=cme;idno=Gawain, accessed April 25, 2012.
9. *Sir Gawain and the Green Knight,* trans. J. Weston. *The Camelot Project* (Rochester, NY: University of Rochester, 1989). Accessed March 14, 2012, http://www.lib.rochester.edu/camelot/sggk.htm.
10. *Sir Gawain and the Green Knight,* trans. W. A. Nielson. *Middle English Series* (Cambridge, ON: In Parenthesis Publications, 1999). Accessed March 21, 2012, http://www.yorku.ca/inpar/sggk_neilson.pdf.

11. *Arthur and Gwain. The Camelot Project* (Rochester, NY: University of Rochester). Accessed April 24, 2012, http://www.lib.rochester.edu/camelot/teams/artgaw.htm.
12. John Lydgate, "The Siege of Thebes," ed. Robert R. Edwards. (Kalamazoo: Medieval Institute Publications, 2001). Available from *The Camelot Project* (Rochester, NY: University of Rochester). Accessed March 31, 2012, http://www.lib.rochester.edu/camelot/thebtx3.htm.
13. *Middle English Dictionary.* University of Michigan. Accessed April 24, 2012, quod.lib.umich.edu/m/med.
14. Jordanus Rufus, *The Care of Horses,* quoted in Steven Muhlberger, *Jousts and Tournaments* (Highland Village, TX: Chivalry Bookshelf, 2010), 37.
15. Ramon Lull, *The Book of Knighthood and Chivalry,* trans William Caxton, ed. Brian R. Price. (Highland Village, TX: The Chivalry Bookshelf, 2001), 77.
16. Ibid., 25–34
17. Chaucer, "The Merchant's Tale," trans. Electronic Literature Foundation, lines 743–4. Accessed March 31, 2012, www.thecanterburytales.org.
18. John Gower, *Cinkante Balades,* trans R. F. Yeager. In *The French Balades,* (Kalamazoo, MI: Medieval Institute Publications, 2011). Available from *The Camelot Project* (Rochester, NY: University of Rochester). Accessed April 25, 2012, http://www.lib.rochester.edu/camelot/teams/yrgfct.htm.